Taylor, Smith & Taylor *Dinnerware*

Lu-Ray Pastels, Chateau Buffet, Empire, Holly & Spruce, and More!

Mark Gonzalez

Schiffer Publishing Ltd

D1712507

4880 Lower Valley Road, Atglen, PA 19310 USA

Acknowledgments

This book could not have been completed without the help and dedication of other Taylor, Smith & Taylor (TST) enthusiasts:

Joe Zacharias
Fran and Carl Stone
Hazel West
Larisa Self
William "Bill" Smith III
Susie and Clifford Beabout
Betty and Jerry King
Steve Sfakis

Items displayed on the front cover include:
Fairway soup bowl with bird decal: $4-6;
Summer Rose covered sugar and creamer: $10-14 set;
Laurel 7" platter with pattern 1178: $8-10;
Scalloped Rim covered butter with blossoms, pattern 651: $15-18;
Pink Versatile dinner plate with thistle decal: $6-8;
Navarre shape covered sugar with heavy gold accents, $5-7.

Published by Schiffer Publishing Ltd.
4880 Lower Valley Road
Atglen, PA 19310
Phone: (610) 593-1777; Fax: (610) 593-2002
E-mail: Info@schifferbooks.com

For the largest selection of fine reference books on this and related subjects, please visit our web site at
www.schifferbooks.com
We are always looking for people to write books on new and related subjects. If you have an idea for a book please contact us at the above address.

This book may be purchased from the publisher.
Include $3.95 for shipping.
Please try your bookstore first.
You may write for a free catalog.

In Europe, Schiffer books are distributed by
Bushwood Books
6 Marksbury Ave.
Kew Gardens
Surrey TW9 4JF England
Phone: 44 (0) 20 8392-8585; Fax: 44 (0) 20 8392-9876
E-mail: info@bushwoodbooks.co.uk
Free postage in the U.K., Europe; air mail at cost.

Copyright © 2004 by Mark Gonzalez
Library of Congress Control Number: 2004100469

Designed by Mark David Bowyer
Type set in Humanist521 BT / Humanist521 BT

ISBN: 0-7643-2071-8
Printed in China
1 2 3 4

Contents

Introduction

The purpose of this book is to showcase the various products made by the Taylor, Smith & Taylor Company from its beginnings in 1899, when it was known as Taylor, Lee & Smith, on into the Anchor Hocking years of the 1970s. During their eighty-two year run, the management, designers, and decorators came up with dozens of unique shapes and hundreds of patterns that separated them from the competition.

A common practice of pottery companies was to use a sequence of numbers to designate their patterns. Some potteries would have hundreds (if not thousands) of available patterns at any given time. The only way to keep track of such a large volume was to assign numbers rather than to refer to specific treatment names. Each pottery had their own system. For example, the Homer Laughlin China Company would designate a pattern based on the shape in which it appeared. Thus, L-618 represents pattern 618 on the Liberty shape. The exact same decal might have been used on their Virginia Rose shape and given the number: VR-288. For each variation and new shape, a new designation was created. In TST's case, there was no letter to designate the shape. TST's pattern 644, known as "Silhouette," was pri-marily used on the Laurel, Empire, and Vogue shapes. In each instance, the pattern is 644 regardless of the shape.

Most of the treatments in this book are identified by numbers. They are official pattern numbers used by TST and not created by the author or other entity.

The only time a pattern number changes is when the same decal is given a different treatment. What this means is a pattern might originally have been used with platinum trim. If that same decal was later used with gold trim, a new number was assigned. For every variation, a new pattern number was created. There are many patterns that were never expanded with variations. There are others, namely Dresden Rose, which have over forty variations, and, therefore over forty pattern numbers.

Among the more confusing variations in pattern numbers are the "halves." If a pattern started out with, for example, platinum trim and was given the number 333, then that same pattern without the trim would be called 333 1/2. There are some treatments that start out without trim, such as 2060, and do not have a 1/2 in the pattern number.

Two pages from a TST company decal book showing four patterns: 1707 — "Myrna" rose with gold stamp border, 1708 — gold stamp border with gold trim, 1709 — border decal with gold edge, and 1710 — small rose sprays with gold trim.

The Taylor, Smith & Taylor Company

The Taylor, Smith & Taylor Company, located in Chester, West Virginia, was in operation from 1899 until 1981. An East Liverpool, Ohio, newspaper, *The Tribune*, ran an article on October 26, 1899 regarding the then new pottery:

> New South Side Pottery
> The articles of incorporation for the new south side pottery has been filed with the Secretary of State at Columbus, Ohio. The incorporators are Colonel John N. Taylor, C. A. Smith, Joseph G. Lee, Albert G. Mason, and William L. Smith. The firm will be known as the Taylor, Lee & Smith Company. It is expected the plant will begin operations about the first of next April.

Construction on the pottery didn't begin until January 25, 1900. In June 1900, the eight kilns were completed and by September 13th, the first pieces were made. The pottery stocked warehouses and began shipping in early 1901. Many of the owners of the new pottery couldn't agree on how the business should be run. In 1901, Lee left the company and the name was officially changed to Taylor, Smith & Taylor in September 17, 1901 to reflect Col. John N. Taylor, Charles A. Smith, and Col. Taylor's sons, Homer Taylor and William L. Taylor. The Smith's would eventually buy out the other shareholders and, by 1906, the Smith family were the sole owners. However, Col. Taylor remained on the board of directors.

Summary of early ownership and management:	
Early Taylor, Lee & Smith management in 1899:	**Early Taylor, Smith & Taylor management:**
Charles A. Smith, president	William L. Smith, president
Joseph G. Lee, vice president	Charles A. Smith, vice president and treasurer
A. G. Mason, secretary	C. C. Davidson, secretary
Homer J. Taylor, treasurer	Colonel Will A. Rhodes, sales manager
William L. Taylor, general manager	W. H. Griggs, general manager

In the early 1900s, it was common practice for potteries to purchase shapes from companies that specialized in modeling dinnerware, kitchenware, and hotel ware. This is one reason many dishes from potteries before 1925 have the same general "look." Taylor, Smith & Taylor's (TST's) shapes from this era include Avona (a copy of a French pottery shape), Latona, Pennova, and Verona. There were also toilet wares, cable shapes (a generic term for plain, heavy body utility ware), and hotel wares.

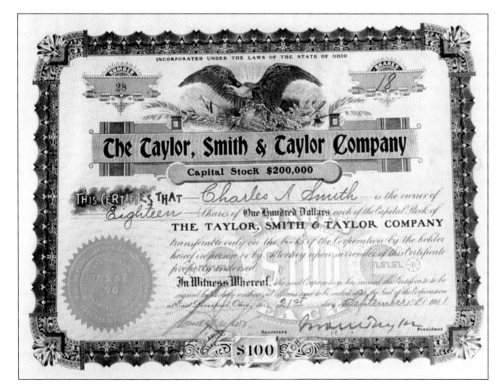

Charles A. Smith's stock certificate from 1901.

Garland plate and Fairway creamer in Depression green glaze. Plate, $6-8; creamer, $3-4.

When American potteries began to come into their own in the 1920s, each started to come up with their own designs — both in terms of shapes and decals — to start competing with each other rather than European imports. Each pottery's shapes and patterns took a unique form. Two of TST's first were Belva and Paramount. It was also during this time TST started to experiment with solid colored glazes such as green, yellow, and a golden amber. Collectors speculate that TST, along with other American potteries, developed these colors to compete with Depression glass, which had become popular in the late 1920s.

Many pottery companies underwent an explosive creative period in the 1930s. Each was competing with each other, which fueled new designs in shapes and decals. TST introduced ten shapes in the '30s — more than in any other decade. They had incorporated the underglaze decoration process with the use of copper plates and rollers that the British had perfected years earlier. In fact, it was through the underglaze decorations that TST came to hire John Plain Thorley, an English potter. Thorley would go on to create many of the more popular shapes and decorations for TST. His contributions helped propel TST into the dinnerware market as a major force. When the Homer Laughlin China Company decided to make underglaze Blue Willow for Woolworth's, they recognized TST's superior underglaze technique and turned to them for help to start their underglaze process.

Early 1950s Montgomery Wards ad featuring Conversation in Lu-Ray glazes, and two Laurel lines with Rose Chintz and Buttercup.

Several changes occurred to TST lines after World War II. Many 1930s TST shapes, such as Fairway, Vistosa, Vogue, and Plymouth, were no longer made. Old deco-styled decals were becoming less popular and were replaced by realistic floral treatments. Square shaped dinnerware was becoming popular in the very late 1940s, and TST produced the Walter Dorwin Teague design, Conversation.

The year 1953 was a turning point in TST's production. The last of the fancy embossed shapes of the 1930s, Garland, was finally discontinued, the more modern, coupe Versatile shape went into mass production. Many of the floral decals created in the 1940s were officially canceled. In comparison, the decals that took their place were abstract and highly stylized. John Gilkes designed many of the shapes and patterns during the 1950s and on into the early 1960s. He is responsible for Versatile, Pebbleford, Ever Yours, and Taylorstone.

The pottery was bought out by Anchor Hocking in 1972. It still operated as Taylor, Smith & Taylor, but according to advertisements of the day, it was, "a division of Anchor Hocking." TST produced durable Ironstone dinnerware until it closed in 1981.

When the company was known as Taylor, Lee and Smith, a general back stamp bearing "Taylor Lee & Smith Co. Porcelain" was used. After the company was reorganized into TST, they adopted a griffin logo. This became a general marking for most of TST's products until circa 1915. Most of the dinnerware produced at the time had its own special back stamp, such as Avona, Pennova, Iona, and Verona. Specialty items and other shapes were given the general "star" marking which consists of the letters TST meeting at the base with a small star. This marking was discontinued when TST started to focus more on dinnerware and less on specialty items in the early 1920s.

The general "shield" back stamp was created in 1930. This was used until 1936 when it was replaced by the "wreath" back stamp. TST wreath marks were used well into the 1960s. Even though these general back stamps were available, many dinnerware lines had their own special markings that contained the shape or pattern name. Examples include: Versatile, Conversation, Lu-Ray Pastels, Coral-Craft, and Pebbleford. By the 1960s, most back stamps contained the name of the particular pattern as well as the shape.

Back stamps often contain a series of numbers indicating a date code. The first single or double digit number represents the month, the second double digit number represents the year, and, if a third number is present, it is a glaze "dipper" number used for quality control purposes. Throughout this book, reference will be made to these general TST markings.

Promotional ad from 1963.

Griffin back stamp.

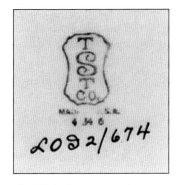

"Shield" back stamp used from 1930 to 1935.

General Taylor, Smith, and Taylor TST marking used from 1936 until circa 1960.

Early TST

This section includes examples from the earliest days of Taylor, Lee & Smith and Taylor, Smith & Taylor. When the company changed owners and names, many of the shapes and decals remained, but the back stamps changed. Most of pieces shown here are vitreous and are marked with the griffin back stamp with the word "vitreous" underneath, while others will have the "star" TST marking used around 1915. The early dinnerware, toilet ware, and cable shapes were discontinued by the mid- to late 1920s when newer shapes such as Belva and Paramount were designed.

Some of the earliest pieces made by TST were decorative specialty items. Plates, plaques, bowls, and other wares were decorated in various tint colors along with gold trim. The decals ranged from fruits, flowers, and roses to Neapolitan, Monks, Grecian figures, as well as cupids, mermaids, and Spanish musicians. Other decorations include heavy cobalt and maroon coloring, elaborate gold tracing, and gold stipple.

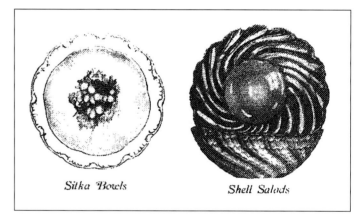

Sitka Bowls   Shell Salads

Parlor Spittoons

Okla

Fargo

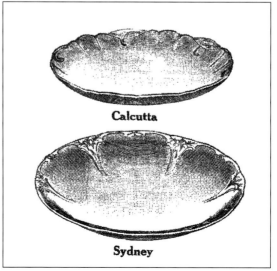

Calcutta

Sydney

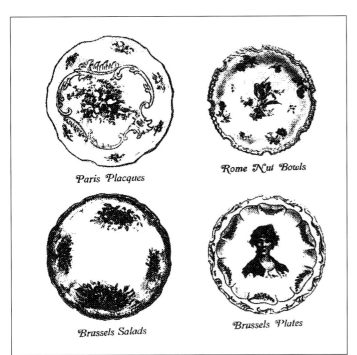

Paris Placques

Rome Nut Bowls

Brussels Salads

Brussels Plates

Dutch jugs from circa 1910. $12-15.

Celery Tray. $10-12.

London Placques

Lace Plates

Cairo Bowls

These drawings come from various TST specialty brochures from before the 1920s and represent a sample of the different elaborate shapes commonly offered by American potteries of the day. Values can be found in the appendix.

Early pitcher, shape
unknown. $8-10.

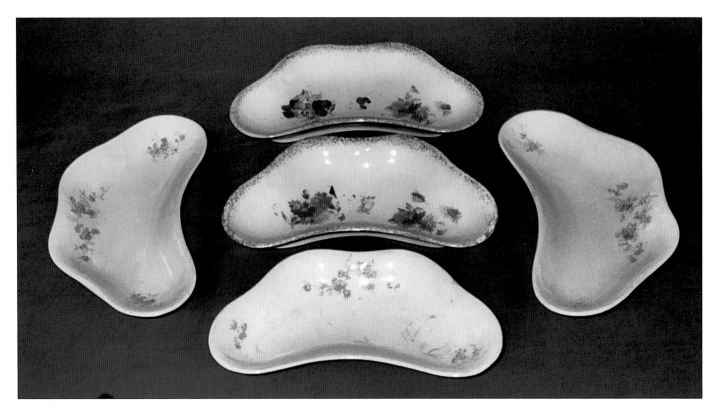

Early bone dishes. $8-10.

The large bowl in the back was one of several TST specialty bowls. It was listed in vintage advertisements as a Florodora Orange Bowls. To the right is an ornately shaped olive dish and in the foreground is a bone dish. The piece to the far left is a cable ware bowl. Florodora bowl, $20-25; olive dish, $10-12; bone dish, $8-10; cable bowl, $4-5.

This casserole is Taylor, Lee and Smith's "Savoy" shape. Its one of the few lines that made the transition to TST so Savoy pieces can be found with both TLS and TST marks. $12-18.

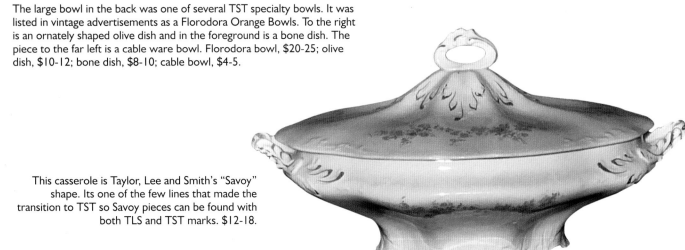

Fish platter. This would have been part of a set that included six or eight 7" plates with similar fish decals. $45-50.

Ad for TST's Navarre and Normandie shapes from circa 1905-1910.

Normandie covered sugar. $5-7.

Normandie covered casserole. $15-20.

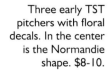

Three early TST pitchers with floral decals. In the center is the Normandie shape. $8-10.

Navarre cup, saucer, 7" plate, and butter pat. Cup
and saucer, $5-7; butter pat, $7-9.

Navarre sauceboat.
$6-8.

Navarre cup and saucer. $7-9.

"Tête-à-Tête" sugar. The Tête-à-Tête shape consisted
of a covered sugar, creamer, and spoon boat. $5-7.

Navarre dishes from a child's tea set.

"*Tête-à-Tête*" spoon boat. $8-10.

Cable ware pitcher. These were made in at least seven different sizes and by both TLS and TST. $8-10.

Assortment of plain cable shapes.

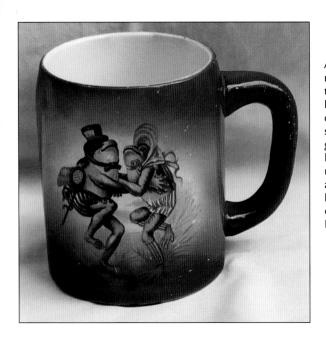

At least two sizes of beer mugs were produced: the Bohemian Jr. and Bohemian Sr. They were decorated with different shaded tints of red, green, and brown. Decals include assortments of monks, frogs, and monkeys. Shown here is one of the frog decals on a brown tinted Bohemian Sr. mug.

Rocaille jugs came in eight sizes and is another piece made by both TLS and TST. The smallest size is 3 1/2 ounces and the largest is 6 pints (or 54s and 6s respectively in trade sizes). The example shown has green tint, but they were also made with blue, pink, and maroon tints. $15-18.

Latona covered jug. $8-10.

Latona demitasse saucer and cable eggcup. The little chick decal was commonly used on children's dishes. Saucer, $1-2; eggcup, $7-9.

Latona tumblers and plate with the "Casino" pattern. Tumbler, $8-10; plate, $7-9.

From the very early 1900s until just before the 1920s, Taylor, Smith & Taylor, like other potteries, sold toilet ware. There were four main shapes: Chicago, Pittsburg (made at a time when there was no "h" in the name Pittsburgh), New York, and a plain shape. None are easy to find, but, of the four, Pittsburg is the most common. Sets are made up of the following: covered soap dish, shaving mug, pitcher, ewer and basin, covered chamber pot, combinet, brush jar, and slop jar. Almost every piece was decorated with floral decals, sprayed on colors, and elaborate gold trim. It is difficult to find a complete set of toilet ware. Usually, a shaving mug or other piece from a particular line is found and misidentified as a piece of dinnerware. Brush jars are often mistaken for vases, shaving mugs as coffee mugs, ewers as service water pitchers, and chamber pots as casseroles!

Chicago juvenile ewer, basin, and chamber pot with baby chicks treatments. Ewer, $25-30; basin, $25-30; chamber pot, $35-40.

Pittsburg shaving mug and ewer. Mug, $8-10; ewer, $15-20.

On the left is a New York toilet shape ewer. It is shown with a Taylor, Lee & Smith pitcher. New York ewer, $15-20; pitcher, $15-18.

Pittsburg shaving mug and brush jar. Mug, $8-10; brush jar, $8-10.

TST's hotel ware was sold under the name "Chester Hotel China." Each piece was marked as such with a circular back stamp. While there were pieces specifically made for the hotel line, many already existing plain and cable shapes made it into the assortment. It is not uncommon to find certain dishes marked with TST's general back stamp and others with the Chester Hotel marking.

An assortment of 24s and 30s "Hall Boy" jugs. $8-10.

A small sampling of Hotel shapes.

Chester Hotel China 9" plate and small platter. Plate, $4-6; platters, $5-7.

Handled and un-handled mustard jars. $10-12.

Compartment plate. $8-10.

Six-compartment, fourteen-inch hospital tray. $10-12.

Small Rocaille jug, cable mug, and ale mug. Jug, $15-18;
cable mug, $3-5; ale mug, $8-10.

Left: poached eggcup; right: Chester shape spittoon. Eggcup, $6-8; spittoon, $10-15.

Hotel ware place setting.

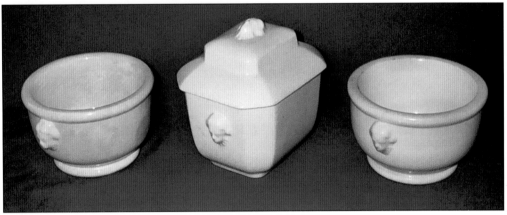

Hotel sugars. Some collectors call these "gargoyle" sugars because of the molded faces. $10-12.

Left: Rocaille jug, right: hotel ewer meant to be sold with a basin. Jug, $15-18; Ewer, $15-20.

TST Dinnerware
Avona

Avona was TST's longest running shape, having first been made around 1915 and remaining in production until the mid-1950s. It was a copy of France's Havilland Ranson shape — a shape copied by many American potteries. TST gave it the name Avona, but Homer Laughlin China (HLC) called theirs, "Republic," Knowles' was "Monterey", and W.S. George's was "Radisson." The decals used on Avona are mainly moss floral sprays very similar to what other potteries used on their own versions of Avona. Some Avona treatments will have simple gold trim whereas others will have the embossing done in solid gold, stipple gold (dapple gold), or with small gold strokes, called "grass" strokes in company records. Avona started out as a very extensive assortment with different sizes of jugs, platters, and casseroles; however, by the end of its production run, Avona had been reduced to the most basic of serving and accessory pieces.

Pansy decal on an Avona 7" plate. The gold decoration on the embossing is called "dapple." A listing of pansy decorations can be found in the decal appendix under the numbers 274, 237, 268, 1432, 1712 (shown), and 1716. $3-4.

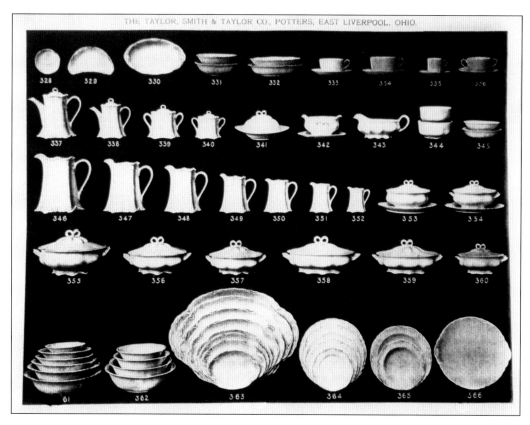

The original assortment for Avona.

Belva

Avona baker with "Bridal Rose" decal and gold trim. $5-7.

Introduced in 1926, the Belva shape was a unique design with hollowware having "stretched" bases and embossing low on the body. This light, raised design was repeated on the verge of flatware. The decals used on Belva were a departure from the norm. The old rose clusters and arts and crafts abstract patterns were replaced with stylized colorful treatments that had an Oriental feel. Bold black trim was used for the first time to accent many of the colorful patterns.

Unfortunately, Belva was not a good seller and was phased out when the more popular Paramount was introduced in 1928. Belva was marked with the "Belva China" name in a horseshoe back stamp.

Belva back stamp.

This pattern is very similar to Bridal Rose, but has a lighter tone. Three official treatments were used on Avona: 1696, with gold "grass etch"; 1715, with gold dapple; and 1743, two-tone body with gold matte lines. One version was created especially for the Empire shape: 1697 with a bright gold edge. $6-8.

Full Belva assortment from 1926.

Avona creamer and sauceboat with pattern 1498. Creamer, $4-5; sauceboat, $6-8.

Pattern 3410. $2-3.

Belva casserole with one of several different "Bird of Paradise" treatments, 3706. $15-20.

Capitol

Capitol was a short-lived line produced from circa 1929 until 1933. The flatware is round with wide rims and the hollowware is conical in form with tab and angular handles. The majority of decorations are "border" decals or simple treatments limited to the rim. The first Capitol back stamp promoted the ivory glaze and featured a dome capitol building with the words "Capitol Ivory." It was common for potteries in the late 1920s to promote their then new and high quality ivory glazes in their back stamps. TST would do so with Iona, Capitol, and Paramount. These markings would become obsolete around 1930 when they were replaced by the more generic TST "shield" marking. In 1931, Rose Mist (pink body) was used on Capitol, Paramount, and Regal. Capitol was discontinued soon after the introduction of Rose Mist.

Indian Tree pattern 3716 with black and yellow trim on the sugar and 24s jug. Pattern 3409 has gold trim and D431, intended for the Paramount shape, has black trim. Sugar, $5-7; jug, $8-10.

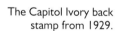 

The Capitol Ivory back stamp from 1929.

Belva 36s bowl with pattern 3713. This was also used on Paramount. $5-6.

Pattern 3023 on the Capitol sugar and creamer. Sugar, $6-8; creamer, $4-6.

Capitol 7" plate. $5-7.

Capitol oval baker with pattern 19. $5-7.

Capitol butter dish with encrusted gold decoration. $10-12.

Capitol sauceboat with pattern 22. $5-7.

Capitol teacup. $4-6.

Capitol fruit cup in Rose Mist body with pattern 321, Orchid. $2-3.

Capitol 24s jug. $10-12.

Special promotional Nestlé's® cup and saucer. This pattern was designated number 1134 and was intended to have maroon trim, but, as the photo shows, pieces were made with no trim. $10-12.

Chateau Buffet

In the 1950s, many potteries were creating buffet ware consisting of coffee carafes, large serving bowls, ice buckets, ramekins, casseroles, and barbecue pieces such as snack plates and mugs. Homer Laughlin had Kenilworth, Roseville had Raymor, and Hall had Flareware. TST's contribution to this new style of ware was Chateau Buffet. The body for the new line was originally made up of iron oxide, but when it proved to be unstable, it was decided to switch to the compound nickel oxide. It is nickel oxide that gives Chateau Buffet its brown color. In order to stand up to heat during use, the body had to have a low expansion rate. The expansion was measured by taking a piece and submerging it in water

for twenty-four hours. If the body didn't absorb water, then it was said to have a 0% expansion rate. With Chateau Buffet, TST was able to achieve the 0% expansion rate.

Any piece that would receive food or liquid, such as the insides of bowls, casseroles, and carafes, was glazed in Pebbleford's speckled turquoise. The brown portion was left unglazed and had a rough texture.

Chateau Buffet was meant to have an old world French feel with modern design. One vintage advertisement claimed the following about the then new line:

> Chateau Buffet in the continental tradition. Old world charm and beauty with a graceful contemporary touch. A subtle blend of cinnamon and turquoise brings warm, quiet charm, while generous vessels evoke the bounty of the castle table. So timeless in its design, yet so modern in serviceability. Chateau Buffet is oven-proof and detergent-proof … an ideal gift item!

Twelve pieces, many of which were given French names, made up the assortment (see values in the appendix for a listing of available items). The Chateau Buffet name was used for a Quaker Oats promotion made by both Taylor, Smith & Taylor and Homer Laughlin. For more on the small promotional set, see the section on Quaker Oats.

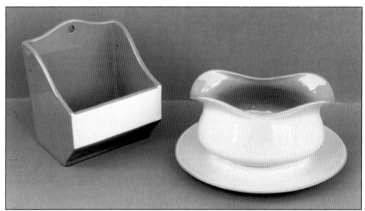
Chateau Buffet salt boxes were made with wooden lids. $18-20. Chateau dinnerware sauceboat fast stand. $6-8.

Chateau Buffet sticker.

Soup tureens were made in two sizes: 4 1/2 quart, "La Grande Terrine" and 2 1/2 quart, "La Terrine Moyenne." Both came with the same brass handle at the end. Later version of the tureens didn't have the handle. $15-20.

Chateau Buffet "Le Saladier" was sold to double as a salad bowl or Boston baker. The spoon and fork are wooden with ceramic handles. $15-20.

Coffee carafe with handle. Sold as "La Carafe," they were often listed in ads with a brass warmer, but without the handle. $10-12.

One of two sizes of Chateau Buffet ashtrays. $12-15.

"Flite-haven" was marketed by TST as Ceramic Bird Shelters. The base clay is identical to what was used for Chateau Buffet with different glaze colors. Shown here is the "Wren Lodge" with a Turquoise Pebbleford top. The ad for Flite-haven states:

> TS&T's exciting new ceramic shelters, styled to catch the fancy of bird-lovers and decorators alike. Created in rich colors ... protected by TS&T's exclusive Zircon-hard Glaze. Solid brass fitting and strong braided Nylon line for hanging. Perfect as bird shelters, smart planters or inspired decorated accessories. Turquoise, Sunburst Yellow or Brown tops; Chateau Cinnamon bottoms."

The turquoise and sunburst colors mentioned are the same used with Pebbleford and the brown is the mahogany color used in two-tone Conversation and Laurel. The suggested retail price was $3.98 and four styles were offered: Wren Lodge, Martin Lodge, Robin Lodge, and Bird Canteen.

"Flite Haven" ad.

Flite Haven Wren Lodge. UND.

Design 70

Design 70 was a dinnerware line based on Chateau Buffet. The body was the same except TST didn't shoot for the 0% expansion rate. Pieces were completely glazed, whereas the brown clay on Chateau Buffet was left exposed. Design 70 was decorated with and without decals and in almost every case, the pattern name is included in the back stamp. Decals were applied to pieces with colored glazes. Just like Chateau Buffet this was done on the exteriors of pieces only, but none of the speckled Pebbleford colors were used. The best selling pattern on green Design 70 was "Lazy Daisy."

From a vintage ad on Design 70:

> Revolutionary ceramic ironware ... a new and different dinnerware ... designed to "go" with the action generation today right into the 70's. Distinctive dimensional patterns ... over locked-in timeless color ... on contemporary mocha bodies set the pace for tomorrow's home furnishing ... fit the mood of today's decor. Choose from 30 coordinated pieces to fit every occasion. And every piece is up to 10% stronger than traditional semi-porcelain; oven-proof and detergent-safe, too. Solid brass and walnut accents.

> Fine American dinnerware for young moderns ... with the bright colors, bold patterns, and appealing shapes. Service a couple or a carload in the best of taste, the most extraordinary practicality. Exclusive new process gives extra strength to body. Oven-proof, detergent-safe ... with colors locked under exclusive TS&T Zircon-Glaze. Dimensional patterns, wood and brass accents make a meal a feast for the eyes!

Design 70 pieces with decals.

Design 70 casserole. This was decorated at the factory by employee Betty Conckle, hence the "BC." It is missing its wooden lid with brass finial.

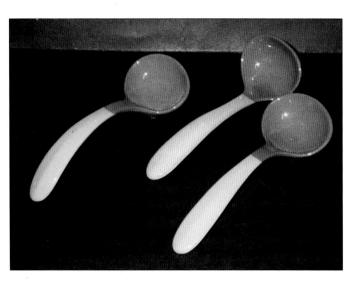

Design 70 ladles. $6-8.

Classic

In the mid-1950s, John Gilkes created a formal line of dinnerware to balance out the casual style of Versatile. The new line, with wide rim flatware and footed hollowware, was named Classic. Three two-tone patterns were made using Classic. "Silver Blue" had two-tone white and turquoise with bold platinum trim, whereas "Heritage Green" was done in two-tone green with thick gold trim. The third pattern, called "Sunburst," was produced in two-tone yellow with gold trim. Other patterns were used on Classic including a gold floral center called "Heirloom."

Classic hollowware was mixed with Versatile flatware to create lines that had a mix of the causal and formal looks. Patterns such as Dwarf Pine, Leaf O' Gold, Fascination, and Moulin Rouge all had Versatile flatware with Classic hollowware.

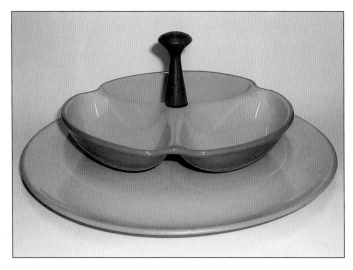

Plate, $4-6 and relish, $8-10.

Classic coffeepot, $15-18 and shakers, $8-10.

Classic sauceboat from "Silver Blue." $6-8.

Classic covered casserole in Lu-Ray's pink glaze. $18-20.

Ads featuring Classic hollowware. Of the three, only Dawn uses the wide-rim Classic flatware. The other two use Versatile flatware mixed with Classic hollowware.

Conversation

After World War II, many American pottery companies started to produce cleaner, more modern shapes to replace the older embossed and deco type dinnerware that was popular in the 1930s and early 1940s. Decals, underglaze prints, and hand-painted decorations were also simplified. TST's first offering based on this new style was the square shape, Conversation.

The flatware had to be made on a jigger. Basically, the top of the plate is made on a mold and the back of the plate is formed by a rotating cutting tool. Clay is put on a mold which creates the "top" or "face." A blade which is manufactured to take on the form of the back of the plate rotates and cuts away the excess clay while at the same time forming the back. This is the primary reason why any square shape flatware will have a round foot. Originally, Conversation's design had corners and edges that were almost perfectly square. This caused a problem when jiggering and the flatware (plates, saucers, and bowls) had to be redesigned with more rounded corners so production could commence. The platter, sauceboat stand, and baker were made on a press and all other pieces were cast.

Many of the treatments originally designed for Conversation involved abstract colorful patterns. Pioneer, Prairie Pheasant, Jamaica, and Coffee Tree were highly stylized. There were also realistic floral decals such as Morning Glory, Daylily, and the very popular, King O' Dell. More often than not, decals were applied to two-tone (TT) Conversation. The rims of flatware, lids to sugars, coffeepots, and casseroles, and exteriors of saucers, cups, creamers, and shakers were all given a contrasting solid color. The three most common are green (also known as avocado), mahogany (dark brown), and coca (light brown). Gray rounds out the four TT colors. Many decals can be found on several different forms of TT Conversation. For example, King O' Dell was sold through the Robison catalog on both green TT and mahogany TT, and while Daylily is commonly found on green TT, pieces with gray TT also show up.

Montgomery Wards sold three Conversations patterns in the 1950s: Prairie Pheasant, Coffee Tree, and Conversation in the Lu-Ray glazes. They originally offered Conversation in the Lu-Ray colors: blue, yellow, gray, and pink. After gray was discontinued in 1953, it was replaced by green. Since Conversation was discontinued in 1954, production of green was much more limited in comparison to the other four colors and is somewhat hard to find today.

Conversation can be found with great ease. The only pieces that may be difficult to locate are the demitasse cups and saucers. Most pieces are marked with the Conversation back stamp, which includes the name of its designer, Walter Dorwin Teague. Once in a while, a large piece of flatware such as a 10" plate or platter will have an overglaze stamp marking of the pattern name.

Swiss Provincial is often found on Sunburst Pebbleford, but was also used on Conversation as shown. $6-8.

"Brittany Peasant" is one of two hand-painted treatments found on Conversation. When treated pieces were mixed with solid brown Conversation, the line was called, "Provincial Fantasy." $6-8.

This is the second hand-painted Conversation treatments, "Mango Seed." Like "Brittany Peasant," its name was changed when sold with pieces in contrasting solid brown to "Modern Fantasy." $3-4.

The "Cockerel" decal was first used on Conversation with five bands, but it would later go on to be used on Versatile in the mid-1950s with a thick cobalt blue band and gold trim. $15-18.

The Conversation demitasse cups and saucers are not particularly easy to find. Here is an example with the "Thistle" decal. $10-12.

One of the more popular decals on Conversation, "Lady Helene," can also be found on Versatile with platinum edge line (2239). It is shown here on TT green Conversation along with "Bahama", pattern 2211, on TT mahogany and solid color shakers. 6" plates, $3-4; shakers, $6-8.

"Pioneer" 10" plate. $6-8.

Pattern 2170: "Petunia". $6-8.

The "Sea Shells" pattern was first developed for use on gray Lu-Ray but Conversation examples are much more plentiful. The treatment here has the Sea Shells decal with lime green trim but there are other versions (see 2061, 2128, and 2222). The decal was also used by W. S. George in the 1950s. Sugar, $8-10; shakers, $6-8.

This rose decal was used by almost every pottery company in the 1950s. TST records refer to this pattern primarily as "Woolworth's Rose" since many TST pieces decorated with the decal were sold exclusively through F. W. Woolworth stores. The Conversation plate with gray band in the back is TST and the nappy, decorated with a dark green band, is the Nautilus shape by Homer Laughlin. TST did the exact same two-tone treatment on their Laurel shape. Plate, $6-8.

Floral decals on a mahogany trimmed 13" platter. $8-10.

Early 1950s Montgomery Ward's ad showing "Prairie Pheasant" and "Coffee Tree" on the Conversation shape. There were two versions of Prairie Pheasant. One is as shown in the ad and the other is the same with the addition of red and green lines encasing the gray band at the rim and a wiggly gray line along the inner rim. Hollow-ware for the second version is usually decorated with bands of all four colors and brown handles. Both versions of Prairie Pheasant are sometimes called, "Prairie Chicken."
Coffee Tree came in several versions; the one shown with Conversation TT green, TT brown, white Conversation with brown edge line (pattern 2127), Conversation TT green with gold trim and encasing line, Lu-Ray Chatham Gray (pattern 2060), and with a simple gold edge line (pattern 2161).

Montgomery Ward's Prairie Pheasant sugar and creamer.
Sugar, $8-10; creamer, $5-7.

"Daylily" on a 6" plate with gray trim and pattern 2186, "Nassau" on a
cocoa trim 10" plate. "Nassau" was also used on the Laurel shape with
mahogany TT and gold lace stamp. 6" plate, $3-4; 10" plate, $6-8.

Prairie Pheasant with added trim lines. $6-8.

"Magnolia" on Conversation chop plate with gray trim. $8-10.

This pattern is called "Jamaica" when on Conversation TT mahogany and "Tropicana" (pattern 2202) when on plain white Conversation. It can also be found with gold trim as pattern 2238. $10-12.

"Colonial Kitchen", a.k.a. "Kitchen Scene", was used in several instances. In the background is a Conversation 10" TT green plate and in the foreground is a Laurel 9" plate with gold lace stamp. Five decals make up the kitchen scenes. Smaller pieces such as cups, sugars, and creamers have decals showing a spinning wheel in front of a fireplace. Larger pieces have decals of colonial women preparing dinner and churning butter. There were at least seven treatments using Colonial Kitchen decals. Pattern 2131 was gold trim and 2167 was a green edge line. The others involve gold lace stamps. $6-8.

Conversation in pastel glazes. Sugar, $8-10; creamer, $5-7.

Two tier tidbit in pink. $10-12

Shown is one of several bird decals used on Conversation 10" plates as special order pieces. Don't expect to find full assortments of dinnerware with these decals. $6-8.

Nappy in yellow, oatmeal in pink, and fruit cup in green. Nappy, $7-9; Oatmeal, $5-6; fruit cup, $3-4.

Ten-inch plates with the "Tropicana" (pattern 2202) treatment and in gray; pink 6" plate. 10" plate, $6-8; 6" plate, $3-4.

Delphian & Beverly

The Delphian shape was created in 1934. It was designed with checkerboard embossing along the rim of flatware and low on the body of hollowware. Sugars, creamers, casseroles, and sauceboats had a high pedestal feet and flowing handles, giving them a fancy, formal look. Delphian was made with underglaze treatments and decals. To date, Delphian has not been found in a solid color glaze or in the Rose Mist pink body available at the time. Delphian was not made for more than two or three years and was overshadowed by its successor, the Beverly shape.

Beverly is a combination of Delphian flatware with redesigned hollowware. Introduced in 1936, the Beverly hollowware had the same embossing as Delphian, but it was placed high at the openings. The new line lacked pedestal feet and ornate handles, resulting in a more casual shape. Beverly finials are thin and flat and most hollowware pieces have four small stub feet. Unlike Delphian, Beverly was in production for almost ten years, being discontinued during World War II.

Six-inch plate with treatment 937 (gold edge line). The platinum version is 738. This decal was also used on the Conversation shape with mahogany two-tone. $3-4.

Nine-inch plate with treatment 1244 1/2. Its parent treatment, 1244, has platinum trim. $5-7.

The checker pattern was used only on Beverly and was hand applied under the glaze. Pieces were meant to have a gold spotted design over the glaze, but examples can be found without the gold decoration. Shown is 1109. The green version is 1110, and red is 1254. Soup, $5-7; creamer, $4-5.

Beverly sauceboat with pattern 1206 with platinum edge. Pattern 1205 uses the same decal with a platinum edge line, pink band, and heavy pink line over the band. $5-7.

Oval baker with pattern 1038 with green trim. Treatment 1246 is of the same decal, but with brown trim. $5-7.

Beverly teapot with gold trim. $18-20.

Pattern 1285 on a Beverly sauceboat. $5-7.

Beverly covered butter dish with rose decals, pattern 696. $20-25.

Delphian sauceboat. This decal is much more common on Vogue. $5-7.

Beverly "Cross Stitch Rose" platter. See patterns 1151, 1271, and 1165 in the appendix. $6-8.

Beverly 7" plate with pattern 1213. Other Petit Point patterns can be found listed in the decal appendix. $4-6.

Beverly "Lace Petit Point" sugar. $6-8.

Beverly plate with red bands. $5-7.

Delphian creamer and teacup with pattern 1017. Creamer, $4-5; teacup, $2-3.

Delphian casserole with pattern 729 and platinum trim. The gold trim version is pattern 696. $15-20.

Empire, created in 1938, was made in a more streamline fashion than Laurel. It had a short body without pedestal feet. Handles were modeled with flowing designs where they came in contact with the body. Lids were made with small bud finials that are difficult to manage. All of the flatware for Empire comes from Laurel: plates, platters, all sizes of bowls, cake plates, lug soups, and saucers. Originally, Empire had its own teacup in the same style as the rest of the hollowware, but it was discontinued early and replaced by the Laurel teacup. The only other piece of hollowware picked up from Laurel is the cream soup cup.

There were four variations of the "Wheel" patterns. Shown is number 576, which is made up of an orange wheel with orange band and platinum trim. The other three are similar in design, but differ in color: 565, green; 566, blue; 577, gray (dark). Normally, the wheels are circular, but on oval platters and baker the design is elongated. $8-10.

Empire & Laurel

Laurel was designed as a plain round shape to replace Capitol in late 1932. It had the same formal style, but the handles were round rather than angular. Finials were knob-like perfect spheres and the insides of the handles were given a small decorative disc — except for casseroles, which were given tootsie roll-like handles. The platters, bakers, lug soups, and cake plates were made with embossed decorative tab extensions.

Both Laurel and Empire were made with decals, banded treatments, and underglaze decorations. The Empire shape was used as a basis for Lu-Ray Pastels. (See section on Lu-Ray for more info.) Because the two shapes overlap in so many ways, treatments meant for one almost always made it to the other. It is not uncommon to find sets, especially from the late 1940s and early '50s, with Empire and Laurel hollowware mixed together. Laurel was discontinued in the mid-1950s, as was Empire in the late 1950s.

Original Empire shape teacup with pattern 644, Silhouette. $12-15.

Sold primarily through Montgomery Wards in the late 1940s, "Rose Chintz" is one of TST's more common underglaze decorations. A multicolored version in black and yellow can also be found, but is not as easy to find as the single colored examples. $6-8.

"Trinidad" on a Laurel rim soup with brown band is pattern 2212. This line was also made with dark green bands. $5-7.

Original Empire shape teacups and saucers with Heatherton decals. This decal was used on several shapes in the 1930s, but when it was used on Empire, it was sold through Sears. The version shown has platinum trim and is pattern 424. The treatment number for Heatherton with gold trim is 412. Cups, $12-15; saucers, $1-2.

Empire sugar and creamer with "Cross Stitch Rose." For more on this decal see the section on Beverly. Sugar, $6-8; creamer, $4-5.

Empire creamer with 1349, Hunt Scene and flat spout teapot with yellow band and gold stamp treatment. Creamer, $4-5; teapot, $20-25.

Empire cup and saucer with the 1930s deco pattern number 840. Hall China's name for this decal is Fuji. $5-7.

Empire shakers with various decal and gold stamp treatments. $8-10 per pair.

Laurel creamer with the fruit basket decal. Pattern 596 has red band and brown drop line as shown and pattern 664 has platinum trim. $4-5.

The "Dresden" rose decal holds the record for the most variations with over forty-five. Shown is "Diana." Dresden Rose patterns are listed in the appendix starting with 1191 and ending at 2052. $6-8.

The 10" plate has the Dresden center decal with blue band and gold stamp design. The smaller plate is done in the same way, but with pink (or "salmon" as TST called it) band and a different center decal. The pattern shown is 1854. In one vintage ad, this pattern was simply called "Bouquet". Listings for this decal are in the appendix under the numbers: 1113, 1190, 1211, 1545, 1684, 1720, 1722, 1771, 1822, 1837, 1838, 1849, 1854, 1855, 1856, 1857, 1889, and 1897. 10" plate, $8-10; 6" plate, $4-5.

There is only one version of this stylized decal: 567 with green band, platinum trim and center decal. Not only are the bands on the rim hand applied, but so is the ring around the decal. The ring is oval on bakers and platters; however, on plates, cups, saucers, etc., the ring is circular. $5-7.

Laurel dinner plate with pattern 674 and platinum trim. Pattern 648, which also has platinum trim, has only the large sprig and pattern 806 has the large sprig but with gold trim. $8-10.

Compartment plate with pattern 781 1/2. The original treatment, 781, was made with green trim. The platinum trim version is 1008. $8-10.

Empire shape demitasse creamer with heavy gold decoration by the Wheeling Decorating Company, a plant in Wheeling, West Virginia, that specialized in decorating pottery and glassware in heavy and ornate gold. $12-15.

The teacup has the dogwood decal which was used in the 1950s. A listing of the various ways it was used is in the decal appendix under the pattern numbers: 2196, 2197, 2203, 2205, 2229, 2230, 2251, and 2252. The dinner plate has a floral cluster with gold stamp and no edge line. Its pattern number is 1921 1/2. There were three main uses of this center decal and various gold stamp borders: 1903, 1921, and 1946. Teacup, $4-5; plate, $8-10.

Empire demitasse set in pearlized glaze and gold trim. Demitasse pot, $40-50; demitasse sugar, $18-20; demitasse creamer, $12-15.

The small double rose cluster was used at least four different ways: 1498 — with the center decal and six floral sprays around the rim (this pattern was done mainly on Plymouth and Avona), 1524 — same as 1498 but on a two-tone body, 1654 — on the Vogue shape with gold design between the swirls, and 1677 with an encrusted gold laurel band along the rim.

In the late 1940s, TST had six treatments that used the pink rose and tulip cluster decal, called "Green Briar." They can be looked up in the decal appendix under 1823 (shown), 1933, 1928, 1945, 1949, and 1991. $5-7.

Laurel covered casserole with blue Dogwood underglaze treatment. $20-25.

Laurel teacup and saucer with brown Dogwood and hand-painted accents. $5-7.

Floral rim decal on a Laurel/Empire dinner plate. Two versions exist: 2093 with gold trim and 2122 on a two-tone body. Since the example shown has no trim, its treatment number is 2093 1/2. $8-10.

Laurel demitasse cup and saucer with pattern 1670. A similar treatment, 1675, makes use of the same rose sprigs, but has a green flange instead of blue. $12-15.

"Wisteria" comes in two forms: 529 with green drop band and platinum trim as shown and 613 with platinum trim. $6-8.

This pattern, 1630, was used on both Vogue and Laurel.

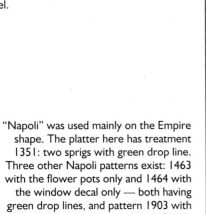

"Napoli" was used mainly on the Empire shape. The platter here has treatment 1351: two sprigs with green drop line. Three other Napoli patterns exist: 1463 with the flower pots only and 1464 with the window decal only — both having green drop lines, and pattern 1903 with both sprigs and red drop line. $8-10.

"Water Lily" 9" and 6" plates. This decal originated on the Plymouth shape, but made its way to Laurel, Empire, and Garland. Pattern 1502 has a green edge line while 1503 is trimmed in platinum. A two-tone version exists as treatment 1529. Two treatments make use of Lu-Ray: 1581 on green with no trim and 1583 on yellow with a green band on the flange. Finally, 1737 has a gold edge line with gold floral stamps along the rim. The Water Lily decal was also used by Homer Laughlin. 9" plate, $6-8; 6" plate, $4-5.

In the mid-1930s, TST produced about a half a dozen decals with Oriental themes. This one, Blue Willow (pattern 503), came only in blue and was not intended to have any trim. While most potteries produced Blue Willow scenes in underglaze form, TST's pattern 503 is a decal. $6-8.

Consisting of six red stamps and two red lines, pattern 1768 is found mainly on Empire and Laurel. Three other colors came before the red stamp/red lines combo: 1761, rose; 1769, violet; and 1746, blue. There is one instance, pattern 1742, where the stamps were used in gold form with a cottage decal and two gold lines. $6-8.

Pattern 1861 with gold trim. Pattern 1860 uses the same decals, but the ware is given a two-tone effect with ivory body and rich yellow shoulder. The treatment is completed with blue edge and verge lines. $8-10.

Laurel shape fast-stand with "Ships" decal. $10-12.

Empire sugar and creamer with pattern 1960. The white, gray, and pink floral decal was used by many potteries in the very late 1940s and early 1950s. Homer Laughlin, Hall, Knowles, W.S. George, and TST all used it on available shapes during that time. TST records list this decal as "Pink Begonia" and they used it at least seven ways: 1952, 1954, 1960, 1972, 1993, 2057, and 2123. See the decal list in the appendix for more information. Sugar, $6-8; creamer, $4-5.

One of the many tulip theme treatments TST used in the late 1930s, pattern 1331 was made in one style as shown: four rim and center sprays with platinum trim. $4-5.

The "Thorny Rose" decal was used five times by TST. The pattern numbers are: 2089, 2088, 1951 (shown), 1955, and 1975. $6-8.

A very popular treatment, Pinecone was first used on Plymouth, but it would go on to be used on Vogue, Laurel, and Empire. These last three shapes with the Pinecone treatments are more available than the Plymouth versions. Pattern 1649 has gold trim and is more common than its counterpart, pattern 1652, which has a green edge line. $6-8.

Yellow calla lilies came in two forms: 1365, gold trim with green drop line and 1367, gold trim as shown. $6-8.

"Marsh Violet," which is much more common on the Conversation shape, is shown here on Laurel lug soups from the early 1950s. The pair shown here has pattern 2209: Marsh Violet decal with green edge and verge lines. There were at least ten uses of the Marsh Violet decal. $5-7.

This Laurel casserole has one of two "encrusted" leaf stamps from the late 1930s-early 1940s. It is pattern 935, complete with a wide gold band, encrusted stamp, and black verge. Many such pieces that have heavy gold decoration were marked "Golden Jubilee", a generic stamp TST used until the mid-1940s. $20-25.

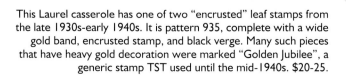

Identical to pattern 935 is the platinum version, 934, on a Laurel 36s bowl. The rim soup has an underglaze stamp decoration in green. Rim soup, $5-7; 36s bowl, $12-15.

TST's name for this pattern was "Holland Mills", but Sears sold it as "Dutch Vista." Its official number is 1398 and can be found primarily on the Empire, Laurel, and Plymouth shapes. $6-8.

Four versions of Autumn Leaves exist: 1215 with red edge line (sets with this pattern are found with either Laurel or Lu-Ray shape teacups); 1214, platinum trim, red drop line followed by brown line; 1218, platinum trim; and 1306, red edge line and brown fine drop line. $13-17.

Laurel sauceboat and Empire creamer with pattern 1519. Sauceboat, $6-8; creamer, $4-5.

Laurel platter with pattern 2228 and yellow fade away trim. $8-10.

This decal is called "Swan Flower" but was sold on dark green TT Laurel and Versatile under the name "Bonnie" as part of TST's Appalachian Heirloom series. Its official treatment number is 2204. Other Swan Flower patterns can be found in the decal appendix under the numbers 2249, 2291, and 2305. $4-5.

Laurel casserole with pattern 1809. Pattern 1749 uses the same decal but has platinum trim. $20-25.

Shown are just two of the twenty-one variations of the cabbage rose decal: 1832 with salmon and gray bands and 1935 with red and gold bands. The other variations are listed in the appendix as numbers: 1789, 1790, 1840, 1868, 1890, 1911, 1926, 1927, 1935, 1936, 1939, 1940, 1941, 1944, 1958, 1961, 1976, 1981, 2094, and 2095. Platter, $5-7; 6" plate, $4-5.

Eggcup with Peasant decal. See patterns 1572, 1578, and 1586 in the decal appendix for descriptions. $7-9.

Shown is pattern 1255 with two sprigs. Pattern 1465 is basically the same with a red drop line, but it has only the larger of the two decals. $5-7.

Empire teapot with red bands, pattern 1997. This treatment, along with patterns 1998, 1999, and 2000 were meant to be used on teapots only. $20-25.

Three versions of this decal exist: pattern 1173 with platinum, yellow, and green bands (as shown); 1174 with platinum trim; and 1199 with green trim. $6-8.

Pattern 2000 on an Empire teapot with curved spout. $15-20.

"Delphian Rose" on Laurel with red band. This underglaze treatment has been found on Delphian, Fairway, and Laurel in red, blue, and green. $6-8.

This Laurel 9" plate has one of the three "Tulip Time" patterns. Shown is 1373 with a red drop line. The other two have blue drop lines; 1363 with two sprigs and 1460 with one sprig. $6-8.

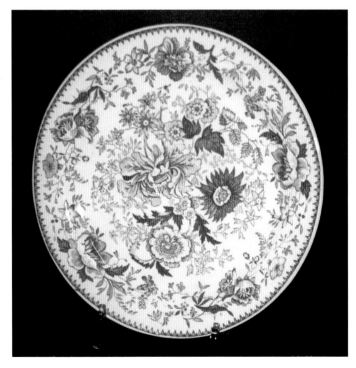

"Center Bouquet" in red. $6-8.

The window box and flower pots combination with red trim is pattern 1216. The window box alone with red trim is pattern 1461 and the flowerpots alone, again with red trim, is pattern 1462. $5-7.

Pattern 682 on a Laurel sugar. $6-8.

At least two names were found in TST records for this decal: "Peasant Rose" and "Floral Bouquet." Pattern 1633 has no trim, 1634 has red trim (as shown), and 1635 has green trim. $6-8.

Laurel platter with floral center decal. Three variations of this pattern exist: 1530 with two-tone body, black verge line, and gold trim; 1569 with blue band (as shown); and 1626 with blue band extending to include the edge. $5-7.

Pattern 1350 on an Empire 10" plate. $8-10.

This decal on an Empire demitasse set was sold on the Plymouth shape as "Miami." Shown is pattern 1479 — Miami with platinum trim and green band. Another treatment using Miami is number 689 with black edge, green band, and yellow line. Demitasse pot, $40-50; demitasse sugar, $18-20; demitasse creamer, $12-15; demitasse cup and saucer, $12-15.

Laurel rim soup and creamer with pattern 745. Soup, $5-7; creamer, $4-5.

"Fifth Avenue" decal on an Empire covered muffin. See patterns 1505, 1506, 1584, and 1579 in the decal appendix for variations. $25-30.

"Rosemont" decal on a two-tone Laurel 7" plate. See the following pattern numbers in the decal index for variations on Rosemont: 2066, 2113, 2130, 2133 (shown), 2185, 2226, and 2290. $5-7.

There are nine variations of the White Flowers treatment which were mainly used on Empire and Plymouth. The Empire sugar and creamer shown are done in coral tones, but they were also done in green. The different patterns for White Flowers is listed in the appendix under 1249, 1250, 1251, 1267 (shown), 1268, 1309, 1338, 1477, and 1478. Sugar, $6-8; creamer, $4-5.

Green Wheat with platinum edge and black verge is pattern 1177. $6-8.

Yellow floral cluster on a Laurel cake plate. There were two official uses of this decal: 1129 with gold trim and 1286 with green edge line. The example shown is from a special cake set that included six 7" plates and a cake lifter with the same decal and gold stamps. $7-9.

"Blue Wheat" comes in two styles: as pattern 1882 with two-tone ivory shoulder and blue encasing lines, and 1180 with platinum trim and black verge line. $6-8.

Red Wheat comes in two styles: 1273 with platinum trim and 1299 with platinum trim and black verge. $5-7.

Empire/Laurel platter with the "Green Flower Basket" treatment and 7" plate with "Daphne." Green Basket was used in four different ways: 1227 with platinum edge and green line; 1228 with platinum edge and green and gray lines; 1269 with platinum edge and green verge (shown); and 1835 with platinum edge and three bands in gray, green, and platinum. "Daphne", known as treatment 1802, is done on a two-tone body with gold trim and body line. It was also sold as "Gold Laurel." Platter, $8-10; 7" plate, $5-7.

Laurel sugar and creamer with pattern 634. Treatment 488 is the same but done in a green tone rather than yellow. Sugar, $6-8; creamer, $4-5.

The Laurel stamp border was used on many different lines. From left to right: Daphne 6" plate; Pebbleford turquoise 10" plate and pattern 1942. 6" plates, $4-5; Pebbleford 10" plate, $10-12.

"Dutch Tulip" underglaze decoration on an Empire footed jug. $20-25.

Wild Poppies can be found on Vogue, Garland, Fairway, and Laurel with red trim as patterns 820 (one sprig) and 829 (two sprigs). Here is a Laurel chop plate with 829 1/2. $10-12.

Empire platter with pattern 1819. $5-7.

Empire teapot with gold stamp and maroon band. $20-25.

This wreath of flowers was used mainly on Plymouth. Here it is on a Laurel 6" plate with platinum edge line as pattern 574. Number 589 is identical with the addition of a green band. $4-5.

Empire juice pitcher, tumbler, sugar, creamer, and shakers decorated with a mother-of-pearl glaze and heavy gold trim. These were more than likely decorated by a smaller outside company who bought "blanks" from TST.

"Acacia" is a common treatment used by several potteries from TST, Hall, and Sebring. TST had three variations: 1484 with gold edge line (this is the more common and most popular); 1881, two-tone ivory shoulder and encasing gold lines; and pattern 2289 on two-tone yellow body. Pattern 1484 was also sold under the name, Chelsea. $10-12.

Underglaze blue and red rose decorations used on the Empire shape. 9" plate, $6-8; 6" plate, $4-5.

Pattern 1850 on fruit cups. The red band version of this treatment is 1851. $3-4.

Laurel sugar and creamer with 1656. This pattern is described in company records as "yellow flange on Laurel with gold encasing lines and gold stamp." There are three others very similar to 1656 and differ only in their flange colors: 1655 (red flange); 1657 (green flange); and 1658 (blue flange). Sugar, $6-8; creamer, $4-5.

Footed Empire jugs with hand-painted blue flowers. The example on the right is complete with dark green leaves while the jug on the left was left unfinished. $20-25.

Hand-painted chop plate. $10-12.

Non-footed Empire jug with hand-painted fruit. $15-20.

This turkey decal was used by many pottery companies. TST put it on Laurel and Lu-Ray platters as well as Conversation platters and chop plates in the early 1950s. $10-12.

Laurel sugar and creamer with "Carnation." Four different treatments included this decal: 1772, 1781, 1782 (shown), and 2123. Sugar, $6-8; creamer, $4-5.

Vintage ads identify this pattern as "Scroll Border", but it was also sold under the names Debutante, Brown Seal, Victoria, and Lorraine. In each instance the pattern number is the same: 1631. Pattern 1797 is the same but done on an ivory two-tone body and 1950 makes use of the same border, but has a bolder floral center. $6-8.

One of the more common treatments on the Laurel shape involves the use of bands and lines in various colors with no other decoration. These were applied to the rims of flatware and the openings of hollowware. Since Laurel was a plain shape, it was perfect for the different banded treatments. The most popular of these was pattern 601, made up of six platinum lines in graduating width along with feet and handles done in solid platinum. One of its predecessors, pattern 555, is the same except the feet and handles were decorated with three fine lines. Treatment 601, called "Sterling" in company records, was almost always used on Laurel, but when Versatile was made in the early 1950s, the two shapes received 601 simultaneously. The treatment was discontinued in the early 1960s making it one of the longest running decorations spanning four decades.

There are over fifty different banded treatments, some of which are simple, such as 1142 with three gold lines; however, some banded treatments can be quite elaborate. Two such examples are 956, made up of nine green and yellow lines, and pattern 957, with a total of ten platinum and yellow lines.

Laurel butter dish with pattern 601. $35-40.

Outside companies would commonly combine dinnerware with metal fittings to make Tidbit trays, snack plates, and bowls. Here a TST Chelsea Chintz underglaze plate with hand-painted accents is transformed into a tray with metal base, handle, and glass knob. $10-12.

Laurel creamer and teacups with pattern 600. $4-5.

Laurel 36s bowl with pattern 555. This treatment is identical to 601 but has a fine line on the foot instead of a solid platinum foot. $12-15.

Empire sugar and creamer with red lines. Sugar, $6-8; creamer, $4-5.

Laurel teapot with yellow and platinum bands, pattern 957. $15-18.

Pattern 728, platinum and blue bands. $8-10.

Though 601 and 600 are very popular patterns, they were not the first ones TST used. The platter and fast stand seen here are decorated in 546: three platinum bands and three gray bands. Pattern 556 is identical except the feet on Laurel hollowware were done in solid platinum. Platter, $5-7; fast stand, $10-12.

Ever Yours

The Ever Yours shape was produced during the 1960s and into the very early 1970s. The shape was made up of Versatile flatware, shakers, and service water jug, Catalina teacup, and pieces designed especially for Ever Yours. The new pieces were the covered sugar, covered casserole, coffee carafe, sauceboat with stand, and divided pickle dish. Several new specialty pieces were offered with Ever Yours: the chip and dip set, the cake plate from Laurel, and a cake lifter or "spatula." The chip and dip set is a combination of a Laurel cake plate with center indention and a dip bowl.

The shape for the new hollowware was streamlined with a slight dropped edge. Creamers had handles that were made part of the body and did not need to be hand applied. Other pieces such as the sugar, casserole, coffee server, and sauceboat were made with no handles at all. The butter dish came from Versatile, but was redesigned without a finial.

Production of Ever Yours overlapped with Pebbleford. Some decaled and plain Pebbleford lines made use of Ever Yours hollowware. The sugar, creamer, pickle, and coffee carafe have been found in the speckled glazes. Ever Yours was also done in solid pastel yellow to coordinate with decaled lines. It is not uncommon to find sugars, creamers, and chip and dip sets in pastel yellow that been separated from their parent decaled sets.

Most of the lines created for Ever Yours were done in two-tone color effects. The insides of hollowware items were often glazed in colors to match the dominant colors in decal prints found on the flatware. Some examples of these include Woodhue with two-tone yellow, Lemon Blossom with two-tone green, Bridal Wreath, Summertime, and Boutonniere with two-tone blue, and Windermere with two-tone pink.

"Pilgrim's Lace" dinner plate. $5-6.

"Brocatelle" dinner plate. $5-6.

"Rose Sachet" cake plate. Hollowware has pink interiors. $7-9.

Background: "Bachelor Button"; Foreground: "Summertime". Both patterns have hollowware with blue interiors. $5-6.

Boutonniere was the most popular pattern on Ever Yours. There were several pick up pieces to expand the set that were not commonly found in other Ever Yours sets. The Laurel rim soup, barbeque set, cereal bowl from Chateau Buffet, and Taylorstone shakers were all decorated with Boutonniere decals. Accessory items were made to go with Boutonniere, namely four sizes of glassware and stainless steel flatware. According to company records, the stainless tableware for Boutonniere included: a hollow handle knife, dinner fork, salad fork, teaspoon, soup spoon, long drink spoon, serving spoon, vegetable serving spoon, salad serving fork, sugar shell, butter knife, and seafood fork. Each piece was individually packed in small plastic bags and twenty-four of each item made up one set.

Ever Yours was marked with a special back stamp. It is with Ever Yours that TST started putting the pattern name in the mark, which makes identification easy today. This practice would continue with most of the remaining TST lines until the company closed in 1981.

"Windermere" cake plate. $7-9.

"Rose Sachet" butter dish. $8-10.

"Woodhue" cake plate. $7-9.

Boutonniere coffee carafe. $12-15.

Boutonniere coffeepot with metal and plastic handle. $15-20.

Boutonniere shakers: the small Versatile shakers were original and were replaced by the larger Ironstone versions in the mid-1960s. $8-10.

Boutonniere Ever Yours sauceboat with stand. $8-10.

Boutonniere cake plate. $7-9.

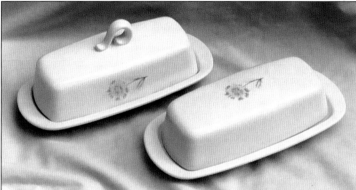

Boutonniere rice bowl and chip and dip bowl. Rice bowl, $5-7; dip bowl, $6-8.

Boutonniere chip and dip set. $15-18.

Boutonniere Versatile butter and plain butter. $8-10, either style.

Boutonniere Ever Yours casserole and brass stand. $12-15.

Boutonniere lug soup. $6-8.

Boutonniere Chateau buffet bowl. $8-10.

Boutonniere rim soup (Laurel/Empire shape). $7-9.

Boutonniere Versatile service jug. $18-20.

Boutonniere Versatile coffeepot. $20-25.

Boutonniere go-along glassware. Any size, $5-8.

Quite possibly the best selling and most collected of TST's underglaze decorations, "English Abby" has been found in red, blue, green, black, and brown. English Abby is often found on Fairway and Garland and with a special back stamp with the pattern name, but no mention of TST or a date code. The Fairway lug soup shown is a somewhat odd design. It was made with three lugs instead of the standard two. $4-6.

Fairway

Fairway was designed with a scalloped edge and light embossing that extended from the rim into the verge. The hollowware was given a scalloped pedestal foot resulting in a formal and antique look. The line was produced from circa 1932 until the mid-1940s. It was a basis for decals and underglaze treatments, but examples have turned up in Depression green and Lu-Ray Pastel colors. The only piece that is found in variations is the sugar. It was made as an "open sugar" and didn't take a lid. These open sugars have a smooth opening without a flange. The lidded version has a flange inside the opening to accept a lid. Fairway will be marked with the two generic back stamps available during its run: the shield mark and the wreath mark.

Fairway casserole with pattern 622. $12-15.

Fairway creamer in Depression green. $3-4.

The platinum stamps on the sugar and creamer shown mimic the embossing. These can be found with and without the monogram letters. The platinum version is 1115 and gold is 1116. Sugar, $7-9; creamer, $3-4.

There are four versions of the "Pansy" flower pot decals shown: Patterns 1344, gold trim; 1369, gold trim and green drop line; 1370, green drop line, gold trim, maroon band, and gold stamp. The cup and saucer example came from a large set of Fairway that had no edge lines. The pattern number in this case is 1344 1/2. $5-8.

This Fairway 9" plate glazed in Lu-Ray's Windsor Blue is unmarked and no information could be found verifying that a standard production line included Fairway in Lu-Ray glazes. Value: UND.

There is no record of this decoration in the TST decal books. It was purchased with Homer Laughlin Virginia Rose 6" and 7" plates with the same treatment. More than likely, this platter, along with the HLC plates, were decorated by an outside company. $8-10.

Fairway oval baker with pattern 716. $5-7.

The "Strawberry" decal was used by Sears on the Plymouth shape. Here it is on Fairway as pattern 1399 1/2. Another version which has a scroll border stamp is 1925. $6-8.

This is the "open" sugar with pattern 557. At some point early in Fairway's production, the base was modified to take a lid. There are two other patterns that make use of this decal: 686 with gold stamps and trim; and 1166 with gold edge line. $7-9.

The gray treatment on the creamer was originally made as pattern 465 with platinum trim and black verge line. Here it is used with no trim lines and it was designated by the company as 465 1/2. (For HLC collectors, this decal was used by Homer Laughlin on their Ravenna shape.) The 10" plate has the underglaze decoration, 712. 10" plate, $6-8; creamer, $3-4.

Fairway platter with pattern 1138 1/2. The normal 1138 treatment calls for gold trim. Two variants of this decal call for three sprigs: 845 with platinum trim and 946 with gold trim. $6-8.

Garland

Garland was designed with a vine embossing around the rim. It was made in the mid-1930s with underglaze treatments, the most popular of which is the castle treatment, "English Abby." Like most other underglaze decorations, English Abby came in a wide array of monochromatic colors including, pink (red), blue, green, black, brown, and mulberry. Besides the underglaze treatments, Garland received decals, and has been found in Depression green and an unusual black glaze. Occasionally, pieces turn up in Rose Mist (pink body) with and without decals, but these are not as common as Rose Mist Paramount, Regal, and Plymouth.

In the very late 1940s, the public's tastes in dinnerware changed from fancy embossed and deco designs to more clean, plain coupe shapes. In March 1953, Garland, TST's last surviving embossed line from the 1930s, was finally discontinued.

There are three uses of the "Modern Morning Glory" decals. The first two were designed to be used on Empire: 1364, three sprays, green edge line, and fine red line; 1366, three sprays and platinum trim. The third style was used mainly on Garland, pattern 1371 with one spray and platinum trim. The no trim example shown would then have the decoration number 1371 1/2. $4-6.

The "Blue Delphinium" treatment was intended for the Garland shape, but it can be found on others, namely Laurel. The pattern number is 1233 and has platinum edge line. However, the 9" plate shown here is the plain trim version: 1233 1/2. $5-7.

The flower basket decal comes in two forms: green with yellow flowers and red with yellow flowers. In total, there are four variations: 718, green decal with black edge line, green band then yellow line; 719, red decal with black edge line, red band then yellow line; 723, green decal and green edge line (as shown); and 777, red decal with orange edge line. $1-2.

Garland 9" plate with pattern 847 1/2. The regular 847 pattern has platinum trim. $5-7.

Pink body (Rose Mist) Garland isn't terribly hard to come by, but it is overshadowed by pink bodied Paramount, Regal, and Plymouth. $5-7.

Pattern 457 on a Garland baker. The gray leaves were originally a deep blue, but have faded over time. $6-8.

English Abby on a Garland teapot. $20-25.

English Abby is common in red and can also be found in blue, green, mulberry, and brown. This black example is somewhat rare. $6-8.

"Briar Rose" with platinum edge was designed for Plymouth, but was used on other shapes such as Laurel and Garland. The two sprig version is pattern 1455 and one sprig is 1456. $6-8.

Handled cake plate with Daisies decal with no trim. Pattern 1023 has yellow trim and 1012 has a green verge line. $7-9.

Blue underglaze decoration on a Garland sugar. $8-10.

The tulip spray pattern had two different names: "Florette" and "Winston." Here it is on a Garland sauceboat and stand with gold stamp on the verge. Patterns using this decal are listed in the appendix under the numbers 1812, 1831, 1913, 1914, and 1922. $8-10.

Garland sugar with pattern 2131. This rose decal was used by almost every pottery company in the 1950s. In TST's case, it was primarily sold through F.W. Woolworth's and, as a result, is often referred to as "Woolworth Rose" in company records. In one instance it is called "Shalimar." $8-10.

Underglaze souvenir plate for the Memorial Gardens of East Liverpool, Ohio. $4-6.

This very unusual black glazed Garland casserole is the only example known at this time. Value: UND.

Fruit cups with blossoms and poppy decals. $1-2.

Granada

The Granada shape was produced in the early 1970s. The wide rim from the flatware was repeated mid-body on the hollowware. Ordinarily, for spatial reasons, flatware decals are larger than those appearing on hollowware; but, with Granada's unique design, the same sized decals were used on both. The early treatments were applied to Granada glazed in muted solid colors of green, yellow, and blue.

One of the first advertisements described Granada :

New from Taylor, Smith & Taylor's "Designer Series" Collection comes this colorful portfolio of flamencan motifs. Inspired by the flavor of Mediterranean handicrafts, these beautiful patterns reflect the artisan's devotion to individuality. No two pieces are identical, each a precious artifact inherited from the potter's wheel. Only TS&T's craftsmanship can lend such fashion to your dining table. Each piece stands as an article to own with pleasure or to give with the assurance of good taste.

The initial offerings on Granada were Matador, Casa Madrid, Mantilla, Casa Verde, and Flor del Sol. Other decorations were used on the Granada shape. Some were done on the solid colors while others were made on a plain white body. Once in a while a piece of solid color Granada can be found without a decal.

"Casa Verde" coffeepot. $10-12.

"Bit of Norway" cup and saucer. $3-5.

Company records indicate this colorful decal was called, "Pattern X." Here it is on a sugar, $6-8, shaker, $7-9, teapot, $15-20, and creamer, $4-6.

Divided serving bowl. $5-8.

Holly & Spruce

Holly & Spruce was first produced in the late 1960s. The flatware was made up of wide rim round shapes and the hollowware was the familiar cylindrical hollowware used in the Taylorstone lines of the 1960s and '70s. A complete list of shapes with values can be found in the appendices.

Order forms from 1968 allowed the buyer to preorder for a September delivery and any order placed before July 1st received 10% off. The original assortment changed very little after its initial release. The tidbit tray had wooden handles at first, but these were replaced by metal versions. An Irish Coffee mug was offered very early, but was discontinued soon after its introduction. The snack set had the shell welled plate with Castilian teacup. These were replaced by a round welled plate and the Cup O' Cheer (punch bowl) cups. Late additions to the line include the covered casserole, Taylor mug, and a Bon-bon dish. The Bon-bon dish is basically a small oval bowl — the only oval shape in the Holly & Spruce line.

Pieces which were large enough to permit it received a Christmas tree decal. These pieces include all the plates, coffeepot, punch bowl, cookie jar, milk jug, Irish Coffee mug, Bon-bon, Deviled Egg plate, Casserole lid, and Taylor mugs. Interestingly, there were no salt and pepper shakers with this line, but there was a Nutmeg shaker. This was nothing more than the regular Ironstone handled shaker with "Nutmeg" spelled out on its side. All other pieces received small holly decals and every piece was trimmed in red.

Holly & Spruce sold very well due to its high quality and reasonable pricing. Cookie jars and coffee pots sold for $3.50 each, creamers and sugars were $1.25 each. A Bowl O' Cheer set retailed for $24.95 and consisted of the 3-quart punch bowl, eight Cup O' Cheer mugs, a nutmeg shaker, plastic ladle, and wooden stand.

The lids to the coffeepot and sugar as well as the handles to the divided relish and original tidbit were made of wood and no doubt products of TST's Timbercraft. Five Timbercraft accessory pieces were offered with Holly & Spruce: The Walnut Party Tray with square tile, a Chip N' Dip Tray with a dip bowl, Cheese Tray with square tile, Candleholders, and a Glass Covered Cheese Tray with round tile. The three tiles all sported the Christmas tree decal and were decorated with a fruit decal on the reverse. The dip bowl was decorated with the holly decal. Candleholders were made with wooden bases and brass tops.

With so many serving pieces (snack sets, a punch set, three ashtrays, and various cups and mugs), it is clear Holly & Spruce was meant to be used at parties and not in the traditional dinnerware manner. The more exotic items, such as the cookie jar, Bon-bon dish, and triangular ashtray, are favorites among collectors and usually command high prices.

An ad showing Holly & Spruce in its later years.

The Holly & Spruce overglaze back stamp.

Milk jug, $15-18 and divided relish, $12-15.

Punch bowl, $12-15 and two cup o' cheer mugs, $4-6.

Cookie jar. $45-50.

Welled snack plate and cup. $12-15.

One of two sizes of round ashtrays. $8-10.

Sugar, $10-12 and creamer, $7-9.

Coffeepot. $30-35.

Nutmeg shaker with a cake lifter. The lifter was not a standard item of the Holly & Spruce line. Shaker, $8-10; Lifter, $7-9.

Deviled egg plate. $20-25.

The following are examples of TST dishes with Christmas theme decals from the 1960s to the 1970s.

Cake plate and handled tray with tree decals not found on Holly & Spruce. Cake plate $6-8; tray, $10-12.

International Brotherhood of Operative Potters promo tray with a listing of officers. $10-12.

Taylor, Smith & Taylor — Anchor Hocking stacking mugs with a special holly decal. $4-6.

International Brotherhood of Operative Potters promo ashtray, $8-10 and mug, $6-8.

The Holly & Spruce tree decal on TST's Octagon shape. This line was sold as "Octagon Holiday." $4-5.

Iona fast stand with pattern 7373. $6-8.

Iona

Iona was a plain round shape first produced by TST in the early 1920s. Shapes were clean without embossing, scalloped edges or other decorative elements. Most of the treatments developed for Iona involve colorful border decals that appeared along the rim of flatware and mid-body on hollowware. Iona was discontinued by the early 1930s.

Iona back stamp from the late 1920s.

Iona casserole. $12-18.

Juvenile China

The Taylor, Smith & Taylor China Company produced juvenile china (children's dishes) for virtually its entire run. Pieces were used from whatever shapes were popular at the time and decorated with decals ranging from people and animals to cartoon characters and flowers. Some of the earliest shapes used were Navarre, Normandie, Avona, Verona, and Iona. There were six initial decorations that made up "Little Hostess Dinner Sets" that could be purchased in thirty-six or forty pieces: Brownies, Tiny Todkins, Kate Greenway Subjects, Edna Pink Rose, Pink Thistle, and Frances Pink Rose.

Iona cup and saucer. $5-7.

Brownies Virginia shape sugars. $20-25.

Iona butter dish base used as a baby plate. $10-12.

Brownies *Tête-à-Tête* sugar. $20-25.

Iona sugar, $5-7 and creamer, $4-5.

From left to right: Brownies Virginia shape creamer, $18-20;
spoon holder, $20-25; and *Tête-à-Tête* creamer, $18-20.

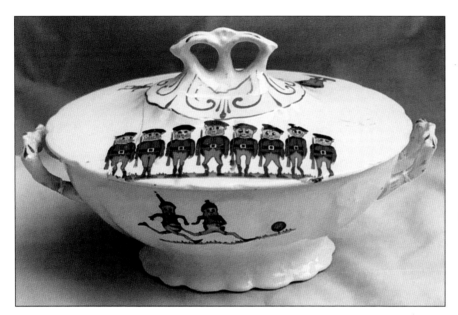

Brownies Navarre shape
small casserole. $85-95.

Brownies Navarre shape
small casserole. $85-95.

Brownies cups and saucers. On the left is the Normandie shape with gold trim and to the right is the Navarre shape without trim. $12-15.

School children Iona sugar, $15-18 and teapot, $60-80.

School children Verona cup, $6-8, saucer, $1-2, and creamer, $10-12.

School children Iona platter, $15-18 and Avona saucer, $1-2.

Verona plate, $8-10 and cable mug
with baby chicks, $10-12.

Tiny Todkins Navarre small casserole. $85-95.

Tiny Todkins Iona creamer, $10-12, plate, $8-10, and 36s bowl, $10-15.

Kate Greenway Navarre cups and saucers. $12-15.

Kate Greenway Navarre platter. $20-25.

Tiny Todkins Normandie plate. $10-12.

Tiny Todkins Iona plate. $10-12.

Latona tumbler, $10-12 and kitty cup and saucer, $7-10.

In the 1930s, TST reduced the numbers in a child's set from the extensive thirty-six to forty piece tea sets to simple breakfast sets consisting of a mug, plate, and bowl. One of the first was a Popeye set from 1937. Howdy Doody was a popular child's breakfast set in the 1950s and by the 1960s other characters were used such as the Peanuts characters, Holly Hobbie, and Raggedy Ann and Andy.

Juvenile China is a hot collectible in its own right. A crossover between collectors occurs with children's dishes, which increases demand and, in turn, increases prices.

Bunting dish. $20-25.

Collectors commonly call these "comic animals." Many potteries used these treatments in the 1930s including Homer Laughlin, Knowles, W.S. George, and TST. $8-10.

Popeye sets were marketed in 1937 and came in four versions. Each three-piece set used the same items and decals, but had different trims and stamp borders. They are listed in the appendix under the pattern numbers: 1135, 1137, 1198, and 1199. Set, $55-70.

Storybook set in its original box. $28-32.

Raggedy Ann and Andy set. $28-32.

The Howdy Doody set was sold through Montgomery Wards in the early 1950s and consist of a coupe shape plate, Chateau Buffet bowl, and a Taylor mug. Set, $55-70.

1950s Prayer set. $28-32.

Holly Hobbie set. $28-32.

Four-piece set of Snoopy mugs in
the Taylor International shape. $10-12.

Suppertime set featuring Peanuts characters. $28-32.

Lu-Ray Pastels

In 1938, TST introduced Lu-Ray Pastels. Named after the Luray Caverns in Luray, Virginia, the line was made up of Empire shapes in four pastel glazes: Windsor Blue, Surf Green, Persian Cream (yellow), and Sharon Pink. The only piece from the original assortment made especially for Lu-Ray was the teacup. Neither the ring handled Laurel cup nor the short-bodied Empire cup was used. The body of the Lu-Ray cup was more flared than the Laurel cup and had a larger, partial handle in comparison to Laurel's small ring handle. The Lu-Ray cup was also used in several decaled lines as an alternative to the Laurel version and collectors today can find marked and unmarked Lu-Ray cups with decals.

A special back stamp was made for Lu-Ray. It usually contains a date code with the month and two-digit year. A third number usually appears for glaze dipping quality purposes. Ordinarily, TST and other potteries didn't mark items such as shakers, teacups, and demitasse cups. Not only were

Lu-Ray shakers and cups marked, but, so were lids to sugars, teapots, casseroles, coffeepots, and the muffin cover lid with "USA." Since TST went out of their way to mark these pieces, it is believed this was done so every piece could be exported to Canada and bear a USA marking.

After Lu-Ray was introduced in 1938, other pottery companies started to make pastel colored lines of dinnerware. Elmhurst Pastels by W.S. George and Serenade by Homer Laughlin were the first and both would become poor sellers in comparison to Lu-Ray. W.S. George would go on to use their pastel glazes on Rainbow and Homer Laughlin used the Serenade glazes on their Nautilus shape for Woolworth's, but neither company could attain the same success as TST. Other pastel lines made to compete with Lu-Ray in the late 1930s and early 1940s include Shenandoah Pastels by Paden City, Camwood and Laurella by Universal, and Deanna by Knowles. Even TST competed with itself by creating "Rainbow" and unmarked line made up of Vogue and Empire shapes in pastel glazes. (See section on Vogue for more information.)

By 1940, TST had become the leader in pastel colored dinnerware. With success came additions to the assortment. The muffin cover, mixing bowls, butter dish, juice set, water tumbler, coaster, and compartment plate were all added by 1942. Unfortunately, the surge in assortment was short-lived. Because of World War II, many potteries had trouble getting oxides necessary in producing colored glazes. Certain items were made in certain colors and, by 1945, many of the more exotic pieces were discontinued altogether. For a listing of the complete assortment with dates of production, see the values section in the appendix.

One reason Lu-Ray's color assortment failed to expand had to do with marketing. The idea was to sell sets in mix colors or "rainbow" sets. Since sets were commonly sold as a service for four or eight, four colors fit the bill perfectly. Once a customer purchased a rainbow set, they could then add serving pieces to their set in any color they desired. With this type of marketing strategy, it was hard to introduce new colors. In 1948, TST did add Chatham Gray to the line, but having an odd number of colors proved to be a failure. By 1953, it was discontinued and the color assortment was reduced to four.

When gray was introduced, it was decided that larger serving pieces would be made in Persian Cream only. These included the salad bowl, water jug, teapot, chop plate, and gravy fast-stand. However, the teapot, chop plate, and salad bowl have all been found in Chatham Gray. Some collectors speculate it is only a matter of time until a water jugs and fast-stands show up in the gray glaze. In the values appendix, these two items in gray are listed with asterisks since their existences are still in question.

In the mid-1950s, the Lu-Ray assortment was reduced to only the most basic serving pieces. It was also during this period that the pastel colored Empire hollowware was being used with Versatile flatware to create a new rimless shape. (For more, see the section on Versatile.) This is one reason why many Lu-Ray hollowware pieces from this time have no back stamps. As unmarked dishes, they could be used with marked Versatile or marked Lu-Ray flatware. The covered casserole and sauceboat, which were discontinued around 1945, were brought back to be used with Versatile in pastel glazes. The 7" Laurel platter was used as a stand for the sauceboat and has been found in Lu-Ray glazes. Most of the time, however, they are found with decals, leading collectors to believe they were meant to be used with the Versatile/Empire combination lines and not part of the official Lu-Ray line. Another questionable piece is the chip and dip tray. Such trays have been found in yellow and pink, but unmarked. Chip and dip trays are the handled cake plates with a center indention to take a small dip bowl. They were created for the Ever Yours lines and are often found with decals. The glazed examples found thus far were probably part of decaled Ever Yours sets that had certain pieces in solid colors to contrast with decals. Collectors will often add the 7" platter and chip and dip tray to their collections since they blend in so well.

In 1961, the Lu-Ray Pastels line was finally discontinued after a twenty-four year run. Because of gray's short production time and poor sales, pieces can be hard to find and prices high as a result. The more exotic serving pieces made in gray command high prices. Items made in the early 1940s such as mixing bowls, vases, juice sets, etc. can also be pricey in collector markets.

Lu-Ray back stamp.

Lu-Ray cups and saucers: regular teacup and saucer in yellow, demitasse cup and saucer in blue, and chocolate cup and saucer in pink.

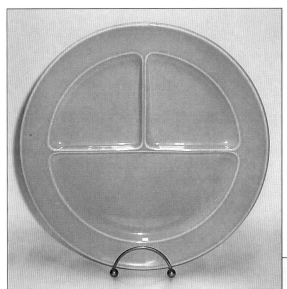

Lu-Ray compartment plate in pink. $30-35.

Lu-Ray 36s bowls: the four original colors are to the left along with four in gray to the right. $55-60; gray, $250+.

Lu-Ray plates in all five colors.

Lu-Ray relish dish in blue. $95-100.

Lu-Ray cream soup cups and liners. Cream soup, $45-50; liners, $18-20.

Lu-Ray lug and rim soups in blue. Lug soup, $18-20; rim soup, $15-18.

Lu-Ray promotional nut dishes or coasters. $95-110.

Lu-Ray eggcups in the four original colors. $25-30.

Lu-Ray juice pitchers. $125-135.

Lu-Ray water and juice tumblers. $70-80.

Lu-Ray pickle in green and the 7" platter in pink. Pickle, $35-50; 7" platter, value UND.

Lu-Ray platters in blue and yellow. $20-22.

Lu-Ray pickle in pink. $35-40.

Lu-Ray sauceboats in the four original colors. $25-30.

Lu-Ray salad bowls in all five colors. $65-70; gray, $250+.

Lu-Ray mixing bowls. $200+.

Lu-Ray demitasse sugars, $65-75 and creamers, $45-50. To view the original Lu-Ray demitasse pieces (commonly called chocolate sets), see the Miscellaneous section towards the end of this book.

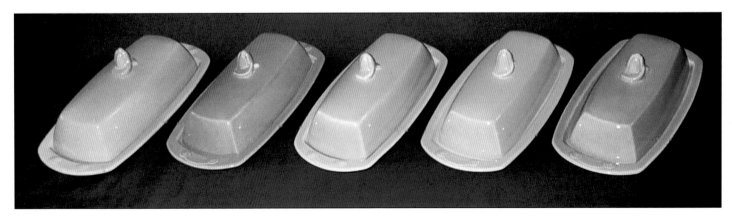

Lu-Ray covered butters. $65-70; gray, $160+.

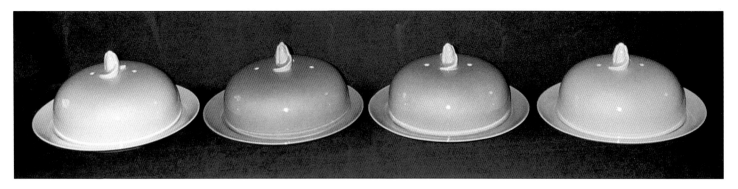

Lu-Ray covered muffins. $110-125.

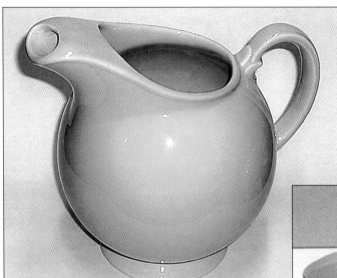

Lu-Ray footed jug in green. $100-125.

Lu-Ray curved spout teapots in all five colors. $85-95; gray, $250+.

Lu-Ray handle-less sugars. $45-50.

Comparison of Lu-Ray teapots: curved spout in gray, $250+; and early flat spout version in pink, $125-145.

Lu-Ray non-footed jug in yellow. $85-100.

Lu-Ray bud vases and flower urns. $250+.

Lu-Ray Flower Vase (Epergne) in green. $250+.

Coral Craft cream soup and liner. $40-45.

Lu-Ray was decorated with decals and banded treatments in the 1940s and early 1950s. The official treatments can be found in the decal appendix. Coral-Craft was a line from 1939 using pink Lu-Ray with one of five white decorations: maple leaf, tulip, laurel, flower border, and Chinese temple. Coral-Craft was not in production for more than a year. There are also pieces of Lu-Ray, as well as other TST dishes, that were decorated by outside companies. These will usually have a second overglaze stamp of the decorator. One of the more common was Atlas China who decorated Lu-Ray with thick platinum bands.

Coral Craft chop plate. $25-30.

Lu-Ray demitasse pots and cups a.k.a. chocolate pots and chocolate cups. The cup second from the left has a white floral decal listed in company records as 1632. For values on Lu-Ray chocolate set pieces, see the values section in the appendix.

Blue Lu-Ray with treatment 1573 yellow deco flower. Other versions of this decal include: 1864 with green band, 1616 with lavender flange, 1556 with yellow band, and 1557 with lavender band. Plate, $12-15; lug soup, $18-20.

Lu-Ray demitasse cups and saucers with treatments. Left to right: Marsh Violet, Chatham Modern, green, and rose bud decal. Cups, $25-30; saucer, $12-15.

Yellow Lu-Ray with treatment 1585. The decal is called "Italian Flora" and was originally created for the Plymouth shape. There were seven other uses and are listed in the appendix under 1544, 1555, 1575, 1615, 1617, 1622, and 1623. $20-22.

"Woolworth Rose" on Lu-Ray Chatham Gray, pattern 2123 1/2.

"Peasant" with brown flange band on a Lu-Ray platter. See the section on Plymouth for more on this decal. $20-22.

Lu-Ray relish dish with rose decals and gold trim. $95-100.

Lu-Ray sugar and creamer with the 601 treatment. Sugar, $22-25; creamer, $10-12.

Lu-Ray flat spout teapot with the 601 treatment. The 601 pattern has been found on the four original Lu-Ray glazes. $125-145.

"Coffee Tree" on Lu-Ray gray. The creamer from this line sports the official treatment number: 2060. For more information on this pattern, see the section on Conversation. Sugar, $22-25; creamer, $10-12.

Lu-Ray casserole with the 601 treatment. $90-110.

"Coffee Tree" treatment 2060 marking on a Lu-Ray Chatham Gray creamer.

"Chatham Modern" in maroon.

Lu-Ray gray with stripes was made in eighteen versions and named "Chatham Modern." The two most common are 2075 in maroon and 2074 in green (shown). See the appendix for a listing of all eighteen patterns.

These Lu-Ray Windsor Blue pieces were decorated by the Atlas China Company with a heavy application of platinum.

Plain Empire and Lu-Ray glazed shakers were used as souvenir pieces for states and landmarks.

TST made calendar plates from the very late 1950s on into the 1970s. Some were made using Lu-Ray and Pebbleford blanks. $10-12.

Early Lu-Ray brochure.

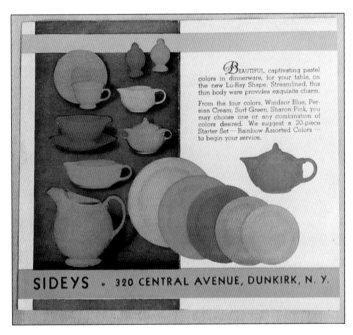

Inside of the early Lu-Ray brochure.

Inside of brochure, circa 1943.

Outsides of the three standard brochures.

Inside of brochure, circa 1948.

Inside of brochure, circa 1955.

Marvel

The Marvel shape was one of the first TST lines to have heavy embossing. It was introduced in the early 1930s and didn't last beyond 1935. The flatware was modeled with embossed roses and slight flutes around the rim. This was also done at the openings of hollowware and the top of the handles.

In late 1932, Quaker Oats approached the Homer Laughlin China Company and TST to make pieces for a breakfast set to be packed in boxes of oats. Quaker Oats never relied solely on one pottery to provide dishes. Ever since the late 1920s, when Quaker Oats offered china products, at least two potteries provided wares. They had used Sebring's Barbara Jane shape and HLC's Trellis in the late 1920s, but by the early 1930s, Quaker Oats was ready for a new shape. Homer Laughlin presented samples of their newest shape, Ravenna; however, Quaker Oats opted instead to go with TST's Marvel. A new name had to be given to the small line made up of the 6" plate, fruit cup, oatmeal bowl, and teacup and saucer. Originally, HLC wanted to call it "Garland", but when it was realized TST already had a shape by that name, "Chelsea" was chosen.

Chelsea is usually marked with the shape name and nothing else. It is not uncommon to find standard sets of Marvel with Chelsea marked pieces mixed in. HLC would go on to make the Marvel 9" plate, platter, and nappy for larger sets to add to their small lineup. They would commonly mix in pieces from their other shapes to fill in the gaps. Orleans, Ravenna, and Virginia Rose, all HLC embossed shapes, can be found mixed with Chelsea to produce large sets of dinnerware.

In 1935, the Marvel hollowware was redesigned. Sugars, creamers, sauceboats, casseroles, butter covers, and teapots were modified with more cylindrical bodies, flat rims at their openings, and the embossing was moved to the bases. The finials were changed to a rose bud that was hand-painted with green leaves and pink flowers. The redesigned Marvel was made primarily for pattern 500, a white and pink floral decal with platinum trim. Records indicate this line was made for five and ten stores.

Platter.

Baker with floral decals and hand-painted embossing. $4-6.

Sauceboat, pattern 433 with platinum edge line. $6-8.

Nine-inch plate with pattern 431. The blue banded version is 1567. $5-7.

Covered casserole, pattern 910. $10-12.

Marvel covered casserole. The decal is called, "Silver Rose" and comes in three treatments. Three sprigs is 335, one sprig is 336, and two sprigs is 337, all of which have platinum trim. $10-12.

Sugar and creamer with underglaze hand-painted embossing in green, pattern 471. Sugar, $5-7; creamer, $4-6.

Sauceboat, pattern 65. $6-8.

Marvel teapot with the Thistle decal is pattern 370. Other Thistle treatments include 347; platinum edge and black fine line, 378; no line with platinum handles, and 380; platinum edge and violet fine line. $30-35.

Pattern 500 on the redesigned Marvel sugar and creamer. Sugar, $8-10; creamer, $6-8.

Octagon

Octagon is a limited assortment, octagonal shape with embossed rim that was produced mainly in the 1970s. The Zircon-hard glaze was touted as being durable and long lasting. The most common pattern, Octagon Amber, has the shapes glazed in a dark gold textured glaze with dark brown accents. Rims of flatware and exteriors of hollowware were given the brown accents. The rose decal from Moulin Rogue and the golden daisy decal from Versatile were used on Octagon. Even the Holly & Spruce Christmas tree decal was used to create "Octagon Holiday." Other patterns include Bridges, Aurora Mist (white with yellow accents), Amber Mist (white with brown accents), and Heritage Mist (plain white Octagon).

Octagon 10" plate with black rim. $4-5.

"Bridges" Octagon 10" plate, $4-5 and 6" plate, $1-2.

Octagon Amber 6" plate. $1-2.

Octagon Amber creamer, $3-4 and shakers, $6-8.

Paramount & Regal

In the late 1920s, American potteries were producing octagon-shaped dinnerware. Homer Laughlin had Yellowstone, Knowles had Marion, and Taylor, Smith & Taylor had Paramount. However, TST's octagon design differed from the others. It was common for potters to make the rim in an octagonal shape and the center well circular. TST's Paramount was done in reverse with a circular perimeter and octagonal well. The flatware was also made with a fancy, embossed rim. The deviation from the norm worked well as Paramount was made from 1928 until 1937, when it was replaced by more modern lines such as Plymouth and Empire.

Paramount's hollowware was made in a low square shape with rounded corners and small molded feet. Handles were angular with small triangular cutout designs on the top and the lugs on many of the pieces of flatware had "holes." These cutouts would have been done when the pottery was in a "green ware" state before firing.

Paramount was one of TST's most extensive lines of the 1930s with a batter jug, syrup pitcher, covered platter, and compartment plate. The patterns used were almost as diverse as the styles of the shapes. At least four solid colors were used: Depression green and pink, a light yellow (sold as "Madrid"), and a light amber glaze. The two Depression colors were done without decals, but Madrid yellow and the light amber glaze (which company records simply called, "colored glaze") were almost always decorated with decals. There is also the Ivory glaze, which is mentioned in Paramount's back stamp from 1928 and 1929. Finally, there is the Rose Mist pink body TST would use during the entire 1930s, first on Paramount, then on Capitol, Regal, Garland, and Plymouth. Most of the Rose Mist and Ivory Paramount was made with decals, though some plain examples can be found. For Rose Mist, the pink color is in the body of the ware. Any piece done in Rose Mist was given a clear glaze so the color would show through.

Regal was introduced in 1931 and was designed with the same embossed border found on Paramount. However, Regal flatware was made in a square design with a circular center well. All the hollowware for Regal is the same as Paramount. Most Regal found today is in Rose Mist with decals and gold stamps. The shape wasn't as successful as Paramount and was discontinued by 1934.

Paramount was marked with a "Paramount Ivory" back stamp in 1928 and 1929. It was then marked with the more generic TST shield marking until 1936 when the wreath back stamp was used. Regal was marked with the shield back stamp.

Paramount creamer in Depression green. $4-6.

Paramount Ivory back stamp on a creamer with its official treatment number D535.

This covered platter comes from a "corn on the cob" set. It is made complete with six 7" plates and a covered butter dish. $20-25.

Paramount compartment plates are not hard to find. This example is decorated with pattern 514. Two similar patterns exist: 137 with a two-tone body and 187 with green trim. There are also early treatment numbers assigned to this pattern: D455 and D498. $10-12.

"Morning Glory" on a Paramount Ivory compartment plate. $10-12.

Paramount Ivory plate with colorful floral decals. This treatment was also used on Marvel. $6-8.

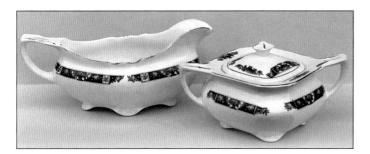

Paramount sauceboat, $8-10 and sugar, $5-8 with blue band decals.

"Yellow Rose" on a Paramount Ivory platter. $8-10.

"Arbutus" is not uncommon on Paramount Ivory. Here it is on a 36s bowl, 9" plate, and teacup. Other variations are listed in the decal appendix as: 211, 221, 246, 261, 280, and 309. Teacup, $4-6; 9" plate, $6-8; 36s bowl, $10-12.

Paramount Ivory fruit cup with two-tone rim and pattern 135. $3-4.

Paramount Rose Mist cream soup with the Thistle pattern. See the section on Marvel for more on Thistle. $6-8.

Paramount Rose Mist baker with pattern 340. The same decals with platinum trim is pattern 462. There was a very similar treatment using green and yellow tones: 341 has a green edge line and gray fine drop line, and 447 has platinum edge. $6-8.

Paramount Ivory covered syrup in pattern 426, 454. $18-20.

Paramount "colored glaze" batter jug with "Gold Tulips." Pattern 144 has gray band (as shown) and 140 has green trim. $20-25.

Paramount Ivory butter dish base with border treatment C402. Butter dish, complete, $12-15.

Paramount "colored glaze" 9" plate and soup bowl. The bowl has the "Hollyhocks" pattern. See treatments 37, 128, and 531 in the appendix for descriptions. $20-25.

Paramount Ivory with green two-tone shoulders and "Bluet" decals. See patterns 209, 220, 244, 245, 318, and 361 in the decal appendix for the uses of Bluet. Cup, $4-6; fruit cup, $3-4.

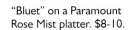

"Bluet" on a Paramount Rose Mist platter. $8-10.

Paramount Rose Mist baker with treatment 259, "French Rose." $5-7.

Paramount Ivory handled tray (without well) decorated with pattern 133 with two-tone rim, black verge line, and gold handles. Pattern 418 uses the same decal but has black handles and no trim. $10-12.

Paramount Ivory handled tray (with octagonal well) used as an advertising piece for Peter Zielinski's Grocery & Meat Market. $12-15.

Paramount covered muffin in Depression pink glaze. $25-30.

Paramount Rose Mist fast-stand with pattern 239 with platinum trim. Pattern 240 is the same but has green trim. $10-12.

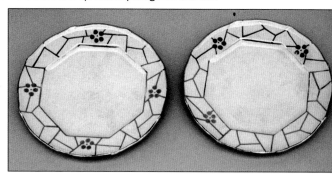

Paramount Rose Mist plates with hand-painted platinum design. $5-6.

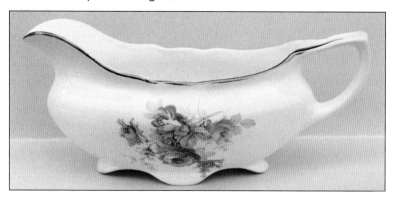

Paramount sauceboat with "Paramount Rose" or pattern 916. $8-10.

Paramount Ivory 7" plate with Morning Glory decals. See patterns 391 and 675 in the appendix for more information. $5-6.

Paramount Rose Mist 9" plate, saucer, and "tall" cup with floral pattern 694. Cup and saucer, $5-8; plate, $6-8.

Madrid (Paramount in light yellow glaze) with pattern 114. $20-25.

Paramount Ivory 9" plate with the colorful "Spring Flowers" decals. See patterns 64, 114, 190, 277, 308, and 629 in the decal appendix. $6-8.

Orange Rose on a Paramount Ivory dinner plate. Patterns that make use of the Orange Rose decal are: 265 with green trim, 267 with gold trim, and 278 with gold connecting line. $6-8.

Paramount Ivory covered syrup with pattern D417. $18-20.

Paramount Rose Mist "Garden" 9" plate with platinum trim (pattern 345). For more uses of the Garden decal, see 346, 369, 416, and 652 in the decal appendix. $6-8.

Paramount Rose Mist covered casserole. $20-25.

Regal Rose Mist 9" plate with pattern 493. $6-8.

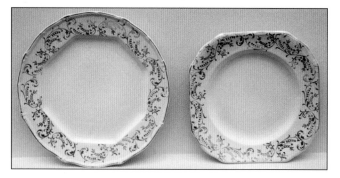

Paramount and Regal Rose Mist plates with gold stamps on the rim. $6-8.

Regal Rose Mist 6" plate with pattern 238 and platinum trim. A black trim version exists as number 351. $4-5.

Regal 9" plate with pattern 403 1/2. There are three standard treatments which all have platinum trim: 403 with three sprigs, 426 with two sprigs, and 454 with one sprig. $6-8.

The "Orchid" decal is common on the pink bodied wares Paramount, Regal, Capitol, Garland, and Plymouth. Here it is shown on the Regal shape. For variations, see patterns 320, 321, 322, 1531, and 1458 in the appendix. $4-5.

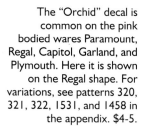

Regal 7" plates with Bird of Paradise decals. $5-6.

Pebbleford

Pebbleford was a solid color line of dinnerware offered from 1953 until circa 1965. The basic shapes used for Pebbleford come from Versatile, but pieces from other lines such as Empire and Ever Yours, as well as specially created pieces can be found. During its early years, it was sold mainly in rainbow sets, but by the end of its production run, it was offered more as single color sets.

Most pieces are marked with a special Pebbleford back stamp with date code. When it was first released, almost every piece was marked, including sugars, creamers, casseroles, etc. But, by the late 1950s, only the larger flatware pieces such as plates and platters were marked. The name, "Gilkes," is often found in Pebbleford markings, referring to the designer of Versatile and Pebbleford, John Gilkes.

The glazes had specks of iron mixed in to give the "pebble" look. Workers who had for years been cleaning up glazes now had to "dirty" them by putting in flecks of iron! The original colors in 1953 were: Sand, Teal, Granite, and Sunburst. Soon after, turquoise, marble, and pink were added. In the late 1950s, sand, teal, and granite were discontinued and a new green, Mint, was added. In the early 1960s, marble and sunburst were dropped and two new colors were added, Burnt Orange and Honey. It was at this time that Pebbleford was sold more as single color sets than in mixed rainbow sets.

Creamer in sand, $6-8; 10" plate in granite, $10-12; and sauceboat in pink, $12-15.

The Pebbleford back stamp.

Pitcher in pink. $35-40.

Covered sugar in burnt orange. $10-12.

Pickle in sunburst, $9-12 and fruit cup in burnt orange, $4-6.

Covered casserole in turquoise. $18-20.

Coffeepots, $30-35.

Ever Yours sugar, $15-18 and creamer, $10-12 in sunburst; covered butter in pink, $18-20; creamer in teal, $6-8; and covered casserole in granite, $18-20.

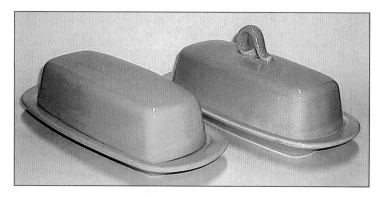

Original butter dish in pink, $18-20 and restyled butter dish in turquoise, $20-25.

Teapot in marble, $40-45; eggcups in sand and yellow, $15-20.

Ever Yours coffee carafe in turquoise. $25-30.

Lug soup, $8-10 and cover, $15-18 in granite.

Taylor Mugs in turquoise. $10-15.

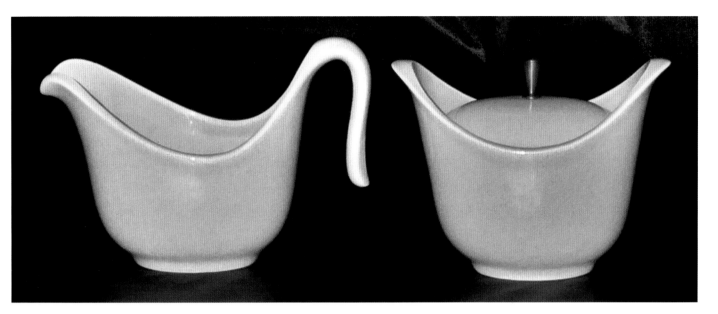

Ever Yours sugar and creamer in honey. Sugar, $15-18; creamer, $10-12.

Pebbleford was used as a decal shape. Most of the time, the decals appear on pieces dipped in turquoise, pink, marble, or sunburst. "Mardi Gras" was made on Pebbleford with contrasting black hollowware, as well as on pink Versatile with Empire hollowware (as shown), and on Pebbleford Marble white and sold as "Hi-Fi."

This wild spiral design was called "String" by TST. It was designed for the Conversation shape, but like so many of the Conversation decals, it made its way on to Versatile and Pebbleford pieces. Here it is on the speckled Pebbleford Marble glaze, but it can also be found on solid pink and blue Versatile flatware and Classic hollowware. String on blue Versatile/Classic was sold as "Beaux Arts." $10-12.

Turquoise Pebbleford with Santa decal and gold stamp border. $10-12.

Turquoise Pebbleford with "White Wheat" which is also found on pastel blue and pink Versatile.

Vintage ad for "Mardi Gras."

Soup tureen and bowls in Pebbleford turquoise with "Artic Night" lid.

"Artic Night" cup and saucer. The flatware for this line is done in Marble Pebbleford with flower design. The hollowware is in contrasting Turquoise Pebbleford. Teacups for these lines are the Catalina shape.

There are three names in company records for this decal shown on a Turquoise Pebbleford casserole lid: Powder Blue, Blue Bouquet, and Twilight Garden.

This Pink Pebbleford casserole with black exterior was done in the same manner as "Mardi Gras." $18-20.

There were at least two other Pebbleford lines offered in the 1950s: "Spice" and "Catalina". Both are excellent examples of a common practice among large potteries: self-competition. The idea is, since another pottery is likely to make an inexpensive copy of a successful line of dinnerware, why not do it yourself? One of the first times TST does this is with "Rainbow," which is nothing more than the Vogue shape in Lu-Ray glazes. It was sold through Montgomery Wards in the very early 1940s as a cheaper alternative to Lu-Ray Pastels. The glazes were identical to Lu-Ray, but the shapes were Vogue (except for two Empire shape pick-up pieces: shakers and footed jugs). TST went out of its way to make sure none of the pieces were marked and the company's name was not used in any of the Rainbow ads. In the 1950s, this method would be applied to Pebbleford to create "Spice" and "Catalina."

Four colors were used to make up Spice: turquoise, granite, sunburst, and pink. The flatware was Versatile, but Empire shape hollowware was used to distinguish it from the standard Versatile hollowware. Today, collectors can find Empire sugars (handle-less versions), creamers, sauceboats, and teacups in these four Pebbleford glazes. Since there was no Empire coffeepot, the standard Versatile coffeepot was used, as were the shakers. Not surprisingly, pieces from sets of Spice (flatware or hollowware) are never marked.

Pennsylvania Dutch decals on Sunburst sugar and creamer. Sugar, $12-15; creamer, $6-8.

Dandelion on pink Pebbleford. $10-12.

Catalina was a little different than Spice. It was distributed through Sunset Potteries of Arcadia, California. Once again, TST went to great lengths to make sure none of the pieces were marked and their name did not appear on any packaging. Catalina shapes include Versatile flatware, the Classic shape coffeepot, and four new pieces: teacup, creamer, tall shaker, and short shaker. These new pieces, later to be called "Catalina shapes" by the company, have elongated "c" shape handles and the creamer and shakers have a stretched look that goes well with the Classic coffeepot.

Three Pebbleford colors were used along with a new green. Usually Pebbleford has the name of the color included in the back stamp; however, since Catalina was never marked, the name of the new green is generally not known. For years collectors have called this color "unnamed green." It did in fact have a name given by TST: Lime Green. The other three standard Pebbleford colors used were renamed as follows: Turquoise to Avalon Blue, Pink to Coral Pink, and Sunburst to Lemon Yellow.

The line was soon repeated with Capistrano, which was identical to Catalina except for the name. Capistrano was sold mainly through the Midwest grocery store chain, Eagle-United, Inc.

Catalina and Capistrano are not terribly rare; but, like Spice, the lack of markings makes it a little harder to find since it is not normally identified by sellers as being related to Pebbleford or TST.

Two examples from Catalina: Classic coffeepot and Catalina creamer in Lime Green. The creamer is odd in that its inside was sprayed with the turquoise glaze. Classic coffeepot, $40-45; Castilian creamer, $10-12.

The four different Pebbleford sugars.

Lime Green Catalina shakers in comparison to the Pebbleford shakers in Mint. $12-15.

Catalina and Pebbleford cups: left front: Pebbleford Granite; left back: Catalina Lime Green; right front: Pebbleford Teal; right back: Pebbleford Mint. Regular cups, $5-8; Castilian teacup, $10-12.

In 1954, a series of accessory items were offered with Pebbleford in plain sunburst or in sunburst with Pennsylvania Dutch and Swiss Provincial decals. They are the four-piece mixing bowl set, four-piece canister set, cookie jar, cigarette box, cheese dish, and Therma-Role. None of the special accessory items have been found in vintage brochures and advertisements. The cheese dish and cigarette box are not uncommon, but the other pieces are somewhat scarce.

At least one cigarette box is know to exist in white with decals. Apparently, the cookie jar, canisters, and Therma-Role were poor sellers since very few examples are found today. The Therma-Role is a "double wall" piece meant to maintain the temperature of its contents. The cookie jar is very similar to the Therma-Role in shape and size, except it lacks the double wall and handles. Canisters are also similar to the Therma-Role, but they have smaller openings and lids in comparison. The Lu-Ray shape mixing bowls were brought out of retirement and dipped in the Pebbleford glazes, sunburst, granite, teal, and sand.

Handle-less sugar in Turquoise from the Spice line, $18-20, and Lime Green baker from Catalina, $15-18.

Pebbleford Mixing bowls in the four original Pebbleford colors. $100+ each.

Catalina shakers in Turquoise (a.k.a. "Avalon Blue"), $12-15.

Left: Therma-Role, $300+; right: cookie jar, $250+. Therma-Roles have handles and are "double walled."

On either side of the Therma-Role and cookie jar are Pebbleford canisters. The one on the extreme left is done in sunburst with "Pennsylvania Dutch" and to the extreme right is "Swiss Provincial." Notice the lids on canisters are smaller than those on the Therma-Role and cookie jar. Values for canisters, UND.

Sunburst mixing bowl with the "Swiss Provincial" decals. $100.

Sunburst mixing bowl with the "Swiss Provincial" decals. $100.

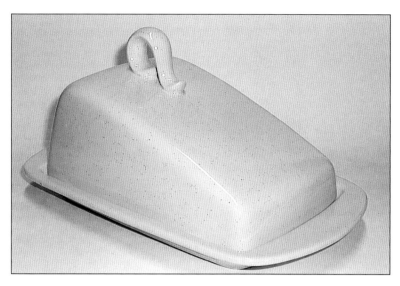

Cheese dish in sunburst. $55-65.

Reveille is a special line of dinnerware with shapes dipped in Pebbleford Honey and decorated with a Rooster decal and red trim. All the flatware is the same coupe shape used in Pebbleford, but the hollowware comes from different lines. Originally, Ever Yours hollowware was used, but by the late 1960s it was replaced by Taylorton shapes. It was also expanded to include accessory items such as triangle ashtrays and cookie jars. Most of the pieces used with the Holly & Spruce line of the same time period were also used with Reveille. In the past few years, demand for Reveille has increased and prices for the more exotic serving pieces have begun to rise.

Pennova

Pennova was introduced circa 1915 and made for only a few years. It had embossing along the rim of flatware and shoulder of hollowware, but unlike its predecessors, Navarre and Normandie, Pennova's embossing was made to have a faint look. On many pieces, one has to look very closely to even see the raised pattern. The decals developed for this shape were also done in a very light manner with dainty flowers in pastel colors.

Reveille dinner plate. $6-8.

Pennova dinner plate. $7-9.

Pennova small jug. $8-10.

tion). One of the more difficult lines to find is Interstate Sunrise Ware (ISW). It is the Plymouth shape in the four original Lu-Ray glazes. Pieces are marked solely "Interstate Sunrise Ware" with no mention of TST.

TST promo card showing Plymouth's original assortment.

Plymouth

In 1937, TST introduced the Plymouth shape. Based on the amount of advertising and promotion, it's clear TST intended this to be their major line of dinnerware. Unfortunately, the line was not a huge success and was overshadowed the following year with the introduction of Empire. Plymouth is a rimless shape (one of the few coupe shapes available to the public at the time). A gadroon embossing was modeled along the rim as well as the finials and handles.

There were several "firsts" in TST dinnerware that occurred with the Plymouth shape. It was the first line not to have oval platters. This would be repeated a year later with Vistosa. Plymouth was the first line to have salt and pepper shakers. The lines that followed, Empire and Vistosa, both had shakers, but oddly, none were created for the existing shapes such as Laurel, Garland, or Fairway. Instead, those lines would pick up the Empire shakers. Finally, Plymouth was given a console set consisting of a pair of candleholders and a centerpiece bowl. Console sets are not common in dinnerware lines and no other TST line, before or after, would have such a set.

Plymouth can be found decorated in three major forms: ivory glaze with decals, pink body — plain or with decals, and underglaze decorations. Most of the decorations created for Plymouth would also be used on Laurel and Empire. Two treatments are found on Plymouth more than any other shape: Mexican Fantasy (a group of Mexican theme decals), and Chinese Temple (an underglaze print decora-

Plymouth pink body shaker, $10-12; covered vegetable, $10-12; and demitasse cup and saucer, $8-10.

All Plymouth is marked with the general TST wreath back stamp. The special "Premier" decal back stamp used for special treatments appeared on many pieces of Plymouth as well as Laurel and Empire.

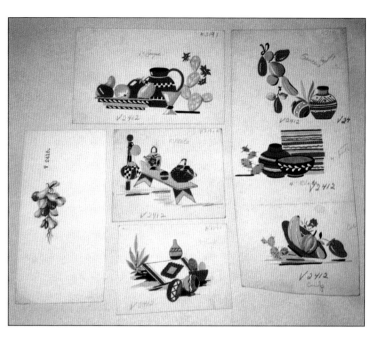

Pattern 1457, "Hyde Park Tulips" with platinum trim, was originally made for Plymouth Ivory, but here it is seen on a Plymouth pink body tray. It was also officially used on Laurel. Pattern 1538 also used the tulips decal but with a red edge line instead. $10-12.

Original drawings for the Mexican Fantasy decals.

"Mexican Fantasy" chop plate and "Adobe" 9" plate. Mexican Fantasy was a series of decals that were used on different pieces within a set. The red trim version is treatment 1510, the blue version is 1511 and Adobe is 1518. Chop plate, $10-12; 9" plate, $6-8.

The "What-not" decal comes in two forms: 1431 with platinum trim and 1466 with blue edge line. Besides Plymouth, the treatments are found also on Laurel and Garland. $6-8.

This pattern is listed in company records as "Barberry." 1514 is the platinum trim version, but its predecessor, pattern 1513, has a red trim. $6-8.

"Duchess", or pattern 1445, is described in company records as "platinum beads between two lines." A second pattern, 1446, was created, this time in gold. Both were originally intended for the Laurel shape, but Plymouth, with its gadroon edge, was favored instead. $10-12.

Plymouth Rose Mist sugar with floral decals. $8-10.

Plymouth teapot with "Rose and Bluebells." $25-30.

Sauceboat and stand with floral decal and black trim. $14-18.

A common and popular treatment: Peasant on a Plymouth 10" plate. This decal was also used on Empire and Lu-Ray. Variations can be found in the decal appendix under 1572, 1578, and 1586. $7-9.

Rose Mist (pink body) Plymouth with the Irises decoration, 1423. According to company files, this pattern was discontinued in mid-1943. Sugar, $8-10; fruit cup, $3-4.

"Dwarf Tulip" comes in three styles: 1512 with platinum trim (as shown), 1535 with gold trim, and 1537 with one sprig and no trim. $5-7.

Lug soups with stylized flowers and red trim. This pattern is 1489; but, when it has platinum trim, it's 1490. $4-6.

A 10" plate with pattern 1636 1/2. The regular 1636 pattern has green band and 1637 has the same decal with a green edge line. $7-9.

Poppy decal on a Plymouth dinner plate. Pattern 1226 uses the decal with platinum trim, so the version shown would be 1226 1/2. The green trim style is 1374. $7-9.

Plymouth fruit cup with pattern 1544. The same decal was used as 1559 but without the maroon band and gold stamp border. $3-4.

Plymouth "Lace Needlepoint" shakers. $10-12.

Plymouth console bowl with "Lace Needlepoint" decal or pattern 1212 1/2. There are other needlepoint treatments listed in the appendix as: 1212, 1213, 1234, 1236, 1253, 1271, 1277, 1718, 1728, 1735, and 1834. $25-30.

Plymouth coaster/ashtrays. $10-12.

ISW cups, saucers, sauceboat and stand, and covered casserole.

Plymouth candleholders. $20-25 pair.

Interstate Sunrise Ware "ISW" flatware in the four Lu-Ray glazes.

Interstate Sunrise Ware open sugar and cup and saucer in Lu-Ray pink.

ISW cake sets come with a chop plate and 7" plates. This particular set was given a stylized floral decal and platinum trim. The decal was also used on Lu-Ray cake sets.

Quaker Oats

Quaker Oats commissioned pottery companies to create breakfast sets in the late 1920s. They would have at least two potteries involved in producing the sets to fill the large orders. Each piece was packed in a box of oats as a promotional give away. The Taylor, Smith & Taylor Company was involved with many of the Quaker Oats products from the late 1920s until the early 1960s.

A breakfast set generally is made up of the following: 6" plate, teacup, saucer, cereal bowl, and fruit cup. One of the first sets was based on Sebring's Barbara Jane shape followed by Homer Laughlin's Trellis and Tudor Rose shapes. (For HLC collectors, Tudor Rose is the same as the Wells shape.) TST shared production of all three of these lines from the late 1920s until circa 1931. In 1932, the TST shape Marvel was used. The small sets were given the special back stamp "Chelsea." For more on Chelsea, see the section on Marvel.

In the late 1930s, Homer Laughlin produced Carnival, a solid color Fiesta-like line for Quaker Oats. There is no evidence that any pottery shared production of this line. TST shared production in three lines that followed, using monochromatic underglaze decorations: Harvest in red, Wild Rose in blue, and Pastoral in green. A special embossed shape created by HLC was used for all three lines and each is marked with appropriate back stamps. The only problem the potteries encountered with the lines was making the underglaze decorations come out the same color so that a piece from one pottery was indistinguishable from the product of the other.

Harvest, the first of the three, was done in red (or "pink" as referred to by the potteries). According to HLC records, this was the only one where TST's and HLC's "pink" wouldn't match properly. It took several trials on both sides to get the final product just right.

The Royal China Company assisted with Wild Rose and produced several larger pieces such as a handled tray, vegetable bowl, sugar, creamer, and dinner plate. HLC made their own version of a 9" plate.

The last of the embossed shapes, Pastoral, is the easiest to find today. TST assigned it the treatment number 1880 and produced it during most of the 1950s. HLC added a 9" plate to the line (the same used with Wild Rose).

In the late 1950s, five shapes were selected from HLC's Oven Serve line to make a special breakfast set: French casserole, cereal bowl, small oval baker, ramekin, and custard cup. These were done in various solid colors; however, this time the colors from each pottery didn't necessarily have to be a perfect match. Some Oven Serve pieces can be found in Pebbleford glazes as well as colors not used in other lines, such as a sage green and mustard yellow. TST and HLC Oven Serve dishes are marked with the appropriate potter's back stamps.

Homer Laughlin's Oven Serve French casserole was made with a bowl and applied handle. TST improved on this design by making the bowl and handle as one piece that could be pressed all at once. HLC did not adopt the TST design and, as a result, two different Oven Serve French casseroles exist.

The Oven Serve name was used by TST a second time in the production of a small set of white body ware with a Rooster pattern.

The French casserole, cereal bowl, ramekin, and custard from TST's Chateau Buffet was made as a small set for Quaker Oats. As with Oven Serve, HLC and TST Chateau Buffet will be found with both potteries' marks. For more on this set, see the section on Chateau Buffet.

Two of the last sets made for Quaker Oats were "Modern Star" and "Fortune." Both were made up of coupe shape 6" plates, fruit cups, oatmeal bowls, and cups and saucers in white with stylized decals. It is not uncommon to find a piece back stamped with the Modern Star or Fortune names with different decals and mixed in with other dinnerware lines as filler.

TST Oven Serve marking.

TST's Oven Serve casserole in green, $3-4 and baker in Pebbleford turquoise, $4-6.

Pastoral bowl. $2-3.

Mother's Oats box with TST and HLC Pastoral.

Mother's Oats box with TST and HLC Oven Serve.

"Rooster" custard, $1-2; 6" plate, $2-3; and fruit cup, $1-2.

Scalloped rim 7" plates with the rose treatment 404 with platinum edge line. Other versions of 404 are: 405, three sprigs with gold trim; 427, two sprigs with gold trim; and 587, one sprig with platinum trim. $4-6 each.

"Rooster" back stamp.

Scalloped Rim

The name "Scalloped Rim" is a descriptive name not officially used by TST. Each piece has an embossed fan, leaf-like design on the rim, and the tops of the handles on the serving pieces have a flower bud. Scalloped Rim was introduced in 1932 as a decal shape, but was discontinued by 1935.

Square shapes were popular in the early 1930s and TST's previous square shape, Regal, had moderate success. Scalloped Rim, on the other hand, did not fare as well.

Expect to find pieces with the TST shield back stamp. To date, no solid color glazed examples, pink body, or underglaze decorations have been found on this short-lived shape.

This 10" dinner plate has pattern 493 with gold trim. The gold stamp, "Give us this day our Daily Bread" is not part of the standard treatment. $6-8.

Baker with pattern 440 1/2. Its parent treatment, 440, has platinum trim. $7-9.

The blossoms pattern, 450, has a good example of a "connecting line" on the verge. The brown line follows the verge and isn't continuous but rather "connects" with the decal. Platinum trim completes the two sprig treatment. Pattern 651 is similar, but has only one sprig and lacks the brown connecting line. $5-7.

Scalloped Rim sugar and creamer. There are three official versions of this decal: 472, one sprig, platinum trim; 473, 2 sprig, platinum trim; and 753, gold stippled edge. The pattern shown is the no trim variant, 473 1/2. Sugar, $7-9; creamer, $4-6.

Treatment 469 is shown here in green with platinum trim. The black version is known as pattern 463. $4-6.

Scalloped Rim soup bowl. $5-7.

Soup bowl, fruit cups, and teacups with the daisies pattern. Descriptions of this decal can be found in the appendix under the treatment numbers: 397, 314, 459, 479, 486, and 494. Soup bowl, $5-7; fruit cup, $1-2; teacup, $4-6.

Shadows

Based on the Classic shape, Shadows was made in 1955. The formal rim shape is accented with an etched flower and vine design. Pieces are usually decorated with green or pink wash colors on the rim to bring the embossing to life, along with gold or platinum encasing lines. The resulting two-tone ware was either left blank or given one of the many decal treatments popular at the time.

Shadows 7" plate with "Kitchen Scene," a.k.a. "Colonial Kitchen." For values, see the section on Classic.

Timbercraft

Timbercraft was a wood making company owned by Taylor, Smith & Taylor, but independently run. In the 1960s, TST purchased an old building located near the pottery. It had been used for several different businesses including a rubber factory and a plastic dinnerware plant. When the building became available, TST bought it with the intent to make crates and pallets. However, there were several employees skilled in woodworking, and it was realized that TST could do more with their wood shop than make simple shipping pieces. After a source for walnut was found, TST started to create different kitchen products such as cheese trays, cutting boards, serving trays, and decorative accessories including candleholders. The new name for their business was Timbercraft.

Timbercraft had good business in the 1960s. Besides creating trays and cutting boards, they also made wooden lids for TST dinnerware lines, namely Taylorton and Taylorstone. The brass finials for these lids were supplied by an outside company. Accents for Chateau Buffet were also made by Timbercraft. This relation ship worked both ways as TST would make tiles for cheese trays. Many tiles (or trivets) were seasonal with fruit decals on one side and Christmas decals on the other. In a very few cases, cutting boards and trays can be found with foil stickers with the Timbercraft name.

Timbercraft cutting board with a Boutonniere trivet. Value: UND.

Verona

Verona, a 1920s line, is very similar to Iona in that both were plain round shapes with few decorative elements. However, Verona does have a slightly more formal look with pedestal feet and stretched handles and finials. The decals also differed; Iona's were narrow bands restricted to the rim whereas Verona's were larger and bolder, having an arts and crafts appearance. Verona must have been a good seller in its day since it is not hard to find. In fact, the different shapes and sizes of casseroles and the bone dishes are readily available.

Verona's full assortment.

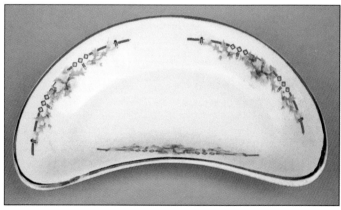

Pattern D424 on a Verona bone dish. $8-10.

Verona sauceboat. $6-8.

Verona sugar, $5-7, and creamer, $4-5.

Verona fast stand. $6-8.

Verona casserole. $12-18.

Versatile

Designed by John Gilkes, Versatile was introduced in 1953. It was created to meet the demand of clean, rimless shapes that became popular in the early 1950s. Traditional handles and finials were not used on casseroles, sugars, teapots, and coffeepots. Instead, pieces were made with tab handle extensions. Not only did this give a contemporary look to Versatile, it also made production more efficient. For example, a lid from Laurel, Garland, or another older shape would have to be made in two pieces: the lid and the finial. They would then have to be joined together with slip clay and fired. With the Versatile design, handles and finials were already part of the lids and bases.

Versatile baker, $7-9; teacup, $2-3; fruit cup, $1-2; and gravy, $7-9, in the 601 pattern, "Sterling." For more on Sterling, see the Empire/Laurel section.

Versatile back stamp.

There are two other Versatile lines which use the coupe shape flatware but mix in hollowware from different lines. These two spin off lines use Empire and Classic hollowware. This results in three distinct forms of Versatile, but there is only one name. It gets complicated since TST would mix the hollowware within a line. A particular set of dinnerware may have Versatile flatware, Empire sugar and sauceboat, and Classic creamer and shakers.

"Marine Life", $5-7.

"Jamaica" on Versatile platter
with yellow fade away trim. $7-9.

"Goldenrod" 6" plate. $1-2.

"Buttercup" on Versatile with
yellow fade away trim. $6-8.

"Strawberry" sugar, $7-9 and creamer, $3-4.

"Shasta Daisy" creamer, $3-4 and sauceboat, $7-9.

Underglaze Blue Dogwood decorations were last used on the Versatile shape after almost twenty-five years in production. $6-8.

These Empire hollow pieces were mixed with pink Versatile flatware with the same decal, "Mardi Gras."

Quite possibly the most common pattern on Versatile, 2308: pastel blue glaze, "Blue Mist" decal and platinum trim. All the hollowware from this line comes from Empire.

"Scandinavian Blue" on pastel blue Versatile. The teacups are from Lu-Ray.

"Scandinavian Blue" on blue Versatile divided baker. $7-9.

These are often referred to as syrups, but they are really creamers that were mainly used in Versatile lines. The example on the left is in the pink speckled glaze from Pebbleford and the one on the right is in Lu-Ray's green. $10-12.

Restyled Empire sugar, $7-9 and tall creamer, $10-12 with pattern 2273, Apple Blossom.

"Winter Scene" on Versatile makes use of Empire hollowware. When it has the cobalt band and gold lace stamp, it's pattern 2257. Other Winter Scenes can be found in the decal appendix under 2258, 2242, and 2243. $3-5.

"Cockerel" on a Versatile coupe soup. This treatment was originally used on Conversation with five gold bands. Here it is decorated with a cobalt band and gold encasing lines. $4-6.

"Blue Claire" on Versatile with a lace stamp. Blue Claire was also sold on two-tone cobalt Versatile. $6-8.

Two patterns that appear on Versatile and use Classic hollowware: "Fascination" on the left and "Moulin Rouge" on the right.

"Silver Mist" 10" plate. Hollowware from this line comes from Classic and is done in two-tone gray. $6-8.

"Golden Day" creamer, $3-4 and sauceboat, $7-9. This line with Black-eyed Susan decals is done on yellow Versatile flatware and Empire hollowware with gold trim.

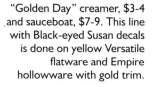

"Leaf O' Gold" is commonly found on white Versatile with gold trim. Here are pastel yellow Empire hollowware examples with the Leaf O' Gold decals and no trim.

Silver Mist was also used on pastel yellow. The teacup here is the special Catalina shape originally made for a spin-off line of Pebbleford. $3-5.

"Buddy Rose" Versatile 10" plate. $6-8.

Versatile serving bowl, $7-9; coupe soup, $4-6; and fruit cup, $1-2, in pastel glazes.

Handled soups that were picked up to be used with the Versatile lines, "Blue Mist" and "Golden Day." $10-12.

The black on the sugar and creamer is meant to accent the underglaze decoration seen on the sugar lid. The snowflakes were put on the flatware and hollowware and received either black interiors (creamer, gravy) or black exteriors (sugar, coffeepot, shakers, etc.). This pattern was sold in various wholesale catalogues as "Midnight." Sugar, $7-9; creamer, $3-4.

To the left is pattern 2210: "Begonia" with green band and gold trim. Other variations include 2240 with gold trim and 2207 Laurel TT green with gold trim. On the right is "Bittersweet" with fleur-de-lis gold stamp. The decal was also used on Classic with turquoise rim and on white Versatile with platinum trim (pattern 2341). $6-8.

Bittersweet on Versatile with Classic shape teacups, pattern 2341. $3-5.

Versatile shakers in amber and white. $6-8.

A 10" plate with Dwarf Pine and 6" plate with Ming. The decals are the same, but the name changes depending on the base color. Plates: 10", $6-8; 6", $1-2.

The Dwarf Pine decal on Classic shape hollowware and Versatile flatware in pastel blue is called "Summer Night." Sauceboat, $7-9; creamer, $3-4.

"Dwarf Pine" on an Empire teacup, $2-3, and Pebbleford turquoise creamer, $4-6.

Dwarf Pine on yellow Versatile is "Ming." Here a Ming platter is used as an advertising piece for a furniture company in South Carolina. Versatile and Lu-Ray platters in the four standard glazes can be found with the Dwarf Pine decal and store advertisements in gold. $8-10.

"White Wheat" on pink Versatile. This decal was also used with Pebbleford's pink and turquoise glazes. $6-8.

Both styles of the Dwarf Pine sugars are easy to find. The bases are the same but the lids differ. On the right is the original flared version used with Classic. The finial and lid had to be made as two separate pieces and then joined together. The restyled lid on the left has a blunt finial resulting in a lid and finial that were made from one piece and saved on production time. $7-9.

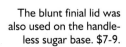

The blunt finial lid was also used on the handle-less sugar base. $7-9.

Empire restyled sugar and Laurel creamer. These pieces with pattern 2252, Dogwood, were found mixed in with Versatile flatware. Sugar, $7-9; creamer, $3-4.

There are two versions of the festoon border seen here. Pattern 1969 is used with gold trim (as shown), and 2119 is done on a two-tone body. Coffeepot, $18-20; sauceboat, $7-9; sugar, $7-9.

Handle-less sugar with "Bachelor Button." $7-9.

This decal was given the somewhat generic name "pink and yellow rose spray" in TST decal records, and was used at least seven different ways. The Versatile pieces with green fade away trim are a departure from the normal yellow fade away trim. Variations of the Pink and Yellow Rose Spray decal are listed in the appendix under the numbers: 1920, 1923, 1947, 2003, 2008, and 2087.

"Petal Lane" cup and saucer. This line uses Versatile flatware and Classic hollowware. $5-8.

"Grape" is a pattern that started out on Conversation. When on Versatile, the flatware and lids to hollowware was done in white with the decal. Bases to hollowware such as sugars, coffeepots, casseroles, etc. were done in the speckled turquoise glaze from Pebbleford. $8-10.

"Spenserian Scroll" was sold exclusively through Montgomery Wards in the early to mid-1950s. $18-20.

These pieces show the three main two-tone colors used on Versatile. The sauceboat is in coral, the coupe soup has cobalt and the sugar has green. The decal is "Golden Wheat" and in some advertisements, the decal on two-tone Versatile is "Regency."

Regency Green (Golden Wheat) creamer, sugar, and shakers. Some sets have white shakers with the Golden Wheat decal on top with gold trim.

Regency Green 10" plate, coupe soup, fruit cup, teacup, and saucer.

"Blue Lace" is made up of Versatile flatware and Classic hollowware, all trimmed in platinum. Flatware was given the decal as was the outside of the creamer and lids to the coffeepot, sugar, and casserole. The exteriors of the sugar, casserole, coffeepot, teacups, and shakers and the interiors of the creamer and sauceboat were given a blue glaze. One vintage ad states this pattern won the "coveted Altman Award for fine design." The line "Pink Lace" is identical, except the blue color in the decal and hollowware are replaced by pink. $8-10.

Yellow Wheat decal on green two-tone Versatile. This decal can also be found on Versatile with gold trim and with yellow fade away trim. $7-9.

"Leaf O' Gold" was decorated in the same manner and has the same assortment as "Blue Lace" and "Pink Lace". The hollowware was decorated in contrasting yellow and each piece was trimmed in gold. $8-10.

One of the earliest types of decorations on Versatile involved spraying trims. Many decaled pieces can be found with yellow or green sprayed trims that were called, "fade away trims" in company records. Several similar trims were used on solid color Versatile. The first was "Mint & Spice," which was made up of solid green pastel Versatile with a light brown spray along the rim. "Cinnamon & Honey" followed and is identical to Mint & Spice except that yellow pastel Versatile was used instead of green. The final two were not as popular and both had the plaid look that was common on dinnerware in the 1950s. "Appalachian Plaid" was done in yellow pastel Versatile with sprayed lines of light brown and blue. Flatware was sprayed in a crisscross plaid fashion and hollowware received the colors on the rim. "Cinnamon Stick", in green pastel Versatile, had an off-center plaid design in light brown. The hollowware for this line was identical to that used in "Mint & Spice."

"Mint & Spice" 13" platter, lug soup, and handle-less sugars with Empire and Classic type lids.

"Cinnamon & Honey" shakers, creamer, sugar base, and casserole.

"Mint & Spice" 10", 8", and 6" plates, cup, and saucer.

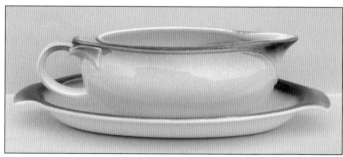

"Cinnamon & Honey" sauceboat and pickle.

"Appalachian Plaid" cups, saucers, and fruit cup.

"Appalachian Plaid" creamer.

"Cinnamon Stick" nappy and fruit cup.

Vistosa

When the Homer Laughlin China Company's Fiesta line gained widespread popularity, other pottery companies started to make their version of brightly colored dinnerware. In late 1937, TST created Vistosa in four bright colored glazes and released it to the public in early 1938. In 1940, a 20-piece starter set, service for four cost $5.76. In comparison, a 24-piece Fiesta service for four ranged between $6.00 and $10.00, depending on the source. Vistosa had moderate success and was discontinued by 1944.

One trade ad from late 1938 said the following about Vistosa:

The richly embossed shoulders of "Vistosa" add a most artistic touch to the flat ware as well as to the bowls and pitchers. Production of "Vistosa", a word derived from the Spanish and meaning "to brighten: to make cheerful" is being stepped up as the new addition to the Taylor, Smith & Taylor Co. pottery gets into full production. The "Vistosa" ware is made in a new addition to the pottery so the gay colors can be controlled accurately throughout the productive process. "Vistosa" ware is for table use at all hours and for all occasions, including regular meals, luncheons and parties. It is produced in bright shades of red, blue, yellow and green. This selection offers the housewife a wide choice of color combinations. Shipment of "Vistosa" ware to department stores has been increasing, including re-orders as a result of the consumer acceptance.

Creamer, $15-20 and sugar, $25-30 in yellow.

Vistosa was given a round shape: flatware was to be circular and hollowware spherical with no ovals such as platters or bakers. Sauceboats are generally elliptical and not spherical so there wasn't one in the original assortment. Demand would eventually make a Vistosa sauceboat possible. The only significant variation collectors may encounter involves the footed salad bowl. The original design called for a ruffled foot, but that was changed to a smooth, rounded foot. While the aesthetics were lost in the redesign, it did simplify its production. The only item that one would expect in a line from the 1930s that wasn't used in Vistosa was the covered casserole. In vintage ads featuring Vistosa, none was ever offered.

Teacup and saucer in cobalt. $15-20.

Lug soup in red. $20-25.

Lug chop plate in green. $35-40.

Hard to find sauceboat in green. $250+.

A 9" plate in cobalt. $15-20.

Smooth foot that replaced the fancy foot version. $200-225.

Ivory glazed Vistosa footed salad bowl with rose and bluebell decals and platinum trim. $250+.

Eggcup in red. $45-60.

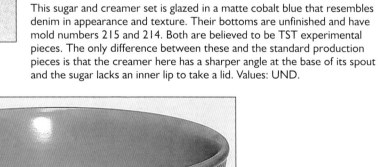

This sugar and creamer set is glazed in a matte cobalt blue that resembles denim in appearance and texture. Their bottoms are unfinished and have mold numbers 215 and 214. Both are believed to be TST experimental pieces. The only difference between these and the standard production pieces is that the creamer here has a sharper angle at the base of its spout and the sugar lacks an inner lip to take a lid. Values: UND.

Footed salad bowl with "fancy" or "ruffled" foot. $250+.

The Vistosa jug has been decorated in Lu-Ray's Windsor Blue glaze — the only example known at this time. The brown shakers are a result of poor firing. The red glaze had to be fired at just the right temperature to come out perfect. If the temperature was too high, most of the glaze would burn up leaving a brown residue as seen on these shakers. Values: UND.

Underglaze green dots on Vogue 9" plates.

Rare decaled Vistosa creamer, pattern 1127 1/2. $15-20.

This oval baker is decorated with pattern 863 — underglaze red dots. $6-8.

Vogue

Vogue was TST's only swirl shape. The rims of flatware and sides of hollowware were all given a heavy embossed teardrop-like swirl. The tops of handles were modeled with an open daisy (a feature that was later repeated on the Vistosa shape.) The line was introduced in 1934 and would continue to be produced for nearly ten years until it was discontinued during World War II in the early 1940s.

Vogue was one of the few shapes to be treated in almost every form of decoration from gold stamps, underglaze prints, hand-painted work, decals, and solid colors. Vogue is somewhat easy to find in today's collector market. Pieces with decals are more common than the other decorations, especially the pastel glazed examples originally made for Montgomery Wards. Expect Vogue to be marked with the general TST shield or wreath back stamps.

The marking for red dots, 863, shows its full pattern number is VOI/863/U.G. with the "V" standing for Vogue, "OI" for Old Ivory, "863" the pattern number, and "U.G." for underglaze.

Vogue chop plate, underglaze decoration. $7-9.

Underglaze hand-painted red leaves decoration. $10-12.

Vogue sugar with the "Shepherdess" treatment which was sold through Sears in the late 1930s. It's shown with a Vogue casserole with and underglaze black decoration. Sugar, $8-10; casserole, $20-25.

Vogue chop plate, underglaze decoration. $7-9.

Vogue chop plate, underglaze decoration. $7-9.

Underglaze red Dogwood on a Vogue 9" plate. The blue and yellow flowers are hand-painted under the glaze. $6-8.

Heathertone, produced from the early 1930s until the mid-1940s, comes in two versions: 412: gold trim and 424: platinum trim. The Platinum trim is much more common and was a good seller for Sears & Roebuck in the late 1930s. Heathertone has been found on TST's Paramount, Vogue, Empire, Fairway, and Laurel shapes. $7-9.

Underglaze red Chinese Temple print with hand-painted blue and yellow accents. $30-35.

Pattern 904 is a yellow floral decal with platinum trim. The no trim version, 904 1/2, is somewhat easier to find. $6-8.

Vogue sauceboat with the "Italian Rose" pattern and blue trim. See the following numbers in the decal appendix for variations on this decal: 582, 628, 1948, 2030, 2031, 2147, 2208, and 2255. $8-10.

Butter dish with pattern 1629. This treatment can also be found on the Delphian shape. $20-25.

Pattern 1542 on the "wide opening" Vogue creamer. $8-10.

There are three different uses of this decal: 1229, with platinum trim (shown); 1230, with platinum, blue, and orange lines; and 1292, with platinum and blue lines. Company records refer to this decal as "Melba." $15-18.

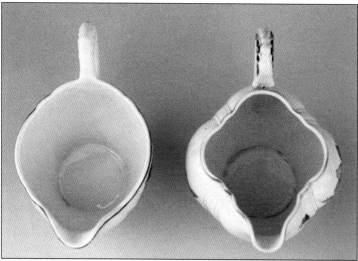

Comparison of the wide opening and regular opening Vogue creamers. Wide opening, $8-10; regular opening, $6-8.

Vogue baker with pattern 821: center house decal with flower border decals. Treatment 1156 is made up of the flower decals on the rim and number 1158 is of the house only. All three are trimmed in platinum. $7-9.

Vogue 6" plates with pattern 1973. Treatment 1783 has gold encasing lines and 1784 has gold trim. $2-3.

Pattern 1164 on a Vogue platter. $10-12.

Pattern 693 on a Vogue baker. $7-9.

Pattern 760.

Treatment 742 on Vogue 9" plate, $6-8 and 6" plate, $2-3.

Vogue teapot in Lu-Ray Pastels'
Sharon Pink glaze. $30-35.

Sauceboat and stand with pattern 708. $15-20.

Vogue 10" plate with "Blue Bell", pattern 1406. Another version exists as 1407. The only difference between the two is that the large pieces of 1406 have two sprigs (or decals) as shown and 1407 has only the larger sprig. $8-10.

Test plate. The number: R-4152 was probably the decal supplier's number. TST's official number for this treatment is 705. A similar pattern in green tones is 703. Value: UND.

Vogue 10" plate with "Southern Belle" decal. $8-10.

1940 Montgomery Ward ad for "Rainbow."

Vogue cups and saucers in the four original Lu-Ray colors. Cup, $4-6; saucer, $1-2.

Later TST Shapes and Patterns

Ranchero was a short set from the 1960s that used Design 70 pieces. It was made with a fade away two-tone glaze in light and dark brown.

Ranchero creamer and sugar. $5-8.

Sierra is a brown drip glaze line made in the very late 1960s to early 1970s to compete with similar lines made by McCoy, Scio, and others. It was made as a short set with only eleven items.

Sierra plates. $4-9.

Heatherton, made in the very late 1960s, consists of plain round coupe shapes not unlike Versatile. It came in four colors: Egg Plant (turquoise), Parsley (green), Radish (white), and Sweet Potato (yellow). Advertisements for this short-lived line stressed its durability, stating, "…oven-safe, detergent-proof, color locked-in will never loose tone or brilliance." Besides being mixed in with the solid color line, Heatherton in Radish was used as a decal shape.

Heatherton 10" plate in "Sweet Potato" yellow. $7-9.

The Taylorton shape was designed by John Gilkes, who also designed Versatile, Pebbleford, and Classic. In the early 1950s, imported fine china became popular. By the late 1950s, American potteries started to produce lines of translucent wares to compete. TST had several, but Taylorton was their most popular.

An advertisement from 1960 said the following regarding Taylorton:

Now, every family in America can enjoy the luxury of fine china. Taylorton is reasonably priced thanks to advanced ceramic research by Taylor, Smith & Taylor. So many ways to use Taylorton, too. Imagine the exotic bread tray as a centerpiece, the sauceboat as a nut dish or candy dish, the pepper mill as a decorative accessory. Dramatic new Taylorton China — graceful, durable, translucent, ovenproof — is your china … For every day, or for the most special occasion. Guaranteed for one year against breakage!

Some of the more common patterns found on Taylorton include: Wild Rice, Echo Dell on white, Echo Dell on two-tone blue, Masterpiece, Ivory Tower (plain white), Happy Talk, Candlelight (same decal as "Fascination" on Versatile), Dianthus, Silver Wheat, Rose Sachet, Rhapsody, and Autumn Splendor.

Taylorstone is a name used to promote the Ironstone lines made by Taylor, Smith & Taylor during the late 1960s and throughout the 1970s. Several shapes were sold under this name using different flatware and hollowware. One of the more popular Taylorstone lines is "Chathay," a modern blue and green design on wide rim flatware.

Other patterns were done on what TST called the "Casual Coupe Shape." These include: Bamboo, Yellow Rose, Sunset, Yorkshire Brown, Yorkshire Green, and Floribunda. Another line of flatware, this time with a slight rolled edge, was called, "Old Town Shape." Patterns on this line include Blue Delft, Yellow Gingham, Mountain Meadow, and Wood Rose. Both the Casual Coupe and Old Town shapes used the same cylindrical hollowware.

The following photos show just some of the many Taylorstone and TST Ironstone lines. The pattern name is often included in the back stamp.

Taylorton ads.

Taylorton relish tray, $8-10 and ashtrays, $4-6.

Taylorstone creamer and covered sugars. $5-8.

Unidentified china body shape sugar and creamer. Both pieces are marked with the general TST laurel back stamp in platinum. Sugar, $6-8; creamer, $5-7.

Persimmon 10" plate. $7-9.

Taylorstone coffeepot. $12-15.

Ten-inch dinner plates: on the left is "Nosegay" and to the right is "Indian Summer." $7-9.

Taylorstone "Cathay" dinner plate. $7-9.

"Colorcraft" is a trade name used by TST in the 1960s. It doesn't refer to a specific line or shape, but rather to the vibrant colors and durability of wares from the time. Most lines using the Colorcraft name are made up of plain round coupe shape flatware with either cylindrical Taylorstone hollowware or the curved body hollowware very similar to the Ever Yours shape. In every Colorcraft line, the flatware was given a pattern and the hollowware and selected pieces of flatware were done in contrasting colors to coordinate with the pattern on the flatware.

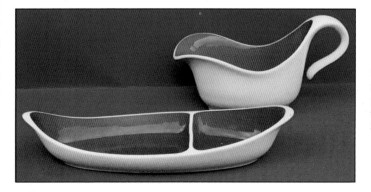

Colorcraft gravy and Ever Yours pickle in two-tone brown. $12-15.

Colorcraft 6" plate. $4-6.

"Shades of Grandeur" was made in the early 1970s. It is a series of four lines using the same underglaze decoration but on different solid colored pieces of cylindrical Taylor Ironstone shapes. Each color was given a special name: blue was "Mediterranean," yellow was "Pharaoh's Gold," coral was "Sahara Sun," and green was "Oasis."

Shades of Grandeur 10" plate, cup and saucer in Oasis green and coupe soup in Sahara Sun glaze. $4-9.

In 1980, Anchor Hocking made a line of kitchenware and dinnerware for Aunt Jenny's. Each piece was given a light beige speckled glaze and decorated with a vintage label

from 1893. TST made a small line of dinnerware with 10" plates having one of four labels: Beans, Chili, Stew, and Hash. Rim soups and mugs were labeled Soup and Coffee respectively. A line of matching glassware was made. Four 6 1/2" glasses with Grape, Plum, Peach, and Apple jelly labels, milk glass mugs with Herb Tea, Hot Cocoa, and Soup, and a set of lidded glass canisters are just some of the glassware items. Though not produced for very long, the Anchor Hocking-TST dinnerware isn't hard to find.

Aunt Jenny's "Chili" dinner plate. $7-9.

Aunt Jenny's coffee mugs. $5-8.

Dogwood was one of TST's last solid color lines of dinnerware. It was sold in the late 1960s in single color sets rather
than in mixed rainbow sets. White and Amber were the original colors, but by 1973 an olive green was added. Each piece
was designed with a heavily embossed dogwood design on a
coupe shape. The finials for lids were done in brass.

Dogwood dinner plate in green. $7-9.

Dogwood dinner plate in white. $7-9.

Miscellaneous TST

The pieces in this section do not necessarily belong to any particular line of TST dinnerware. Some are promotional or special items made during TST's production run.

The soup tureen was a product of the late 1940s and early 1950s. It was not part of a standard dinnerware line, but rather was classified by TST as a piece of "Art Ware." Most of the popular decals of the day were used on the tureen namely Buttercup (shown) and Italian Rose. The lids have a notch cut out at the edge to allow for a ladle. $20-25.

Here the soup tureen is decorated with the Italian Rose decals. $20-25.

The cigarette box was made circa 1953-54. When found, they are almost always in the Pebbleford Sunburst glaze, but here is an example with Conversation's "Meadow Tree" decals. $25-30.

In the late 1940s and early '50s, TST produced an apple line of kitchenware. It included four pieces: a cookie jar, grease jar, range salt shaker, and range pepper shaker. Since these pieces are almost always unmarked, dealers tend to attribute them to other companies such as McCoy and Hull. Shown here are the three pieces of the "range set," the grease jar and shakers. As with the cookie jar, which is just a larger version of the grease jar, they are glazed in pastel yellow with overglaze red and green coloring. The red was sprayed on and the green was hand-painted to give detail to the leaves. All four pieces are rather easy to find today, but because they are commonly misidentified as being products of the more expensive art potteries, they are usually overpriced.

Apple range shakers, $20-35 and grease jar, $25-30.

State plates are very common. They were made primarily in the 1950s on Laurel, Conversation, and Versatile blanks. The one shown has simple gold band decorations, but most of the time there are heavy gold lace stamps along the rim. One collector reports having state plates for every state except Alaska and Hawaii.

South Carolina state plate. $7-10.

In the 1950s, TST made a set of Howdy Doody children's dishes (see the section on Juvenile China) and the Purinton Pottery made Howdy Doody cookie jars and banks. While there was never an official business relationship between Purinton and TST, the two potteries would often work together. Some of the Howdy Doody cookie jars were made at TST.

Howdy Doody cookie jar. $250+.

Leaf Fantasy snack sets were made by both TST and Universal Potteries in the early 1950s. TST used four of the five Lu-Ray colors: gray, green, yellow, and pink. Universal made the same sets in their own pastel glazes that are not easily confused with TST's. Moreover, both potteries used their own Leaf Fantasy back stamps.

Leaf Fantasy snack set. $25-32.

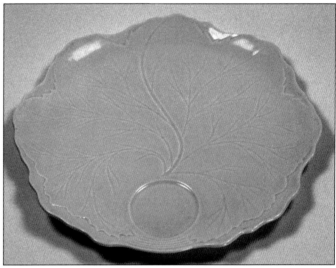

Leaf Fantasy snack plate. $15-20.

George and Martha. $10-12.

George and Martha Washington decals were put on different sizes of Laurel and Conversation plates and platters, with and without gold stamp borders. The two shown here were made as promotional pieces for Mt. Vernon.

In the section on Lu-Ray Pastels, there's a picture of Lu-Ray glazed shakers with souvenir decals. The same treatments were also applied to ashtrays made at TST. Unfortunately, the ashtrays were not marked. They can be distinguished by the light panel embossing on the rim.

Many TST ashtrays, as well as those by other potteries, have risqué jokes. They come from the 1950s and many are sexist and racist and would never be produced today. TST employees state these particular ashtrays were decorated by an outside decorating company.

Promotional coasters with Pottery Festival and National Brotherhood Operative Potters gold stamps. $6-8.

Souvenir ashtrays. $5-8.

Naughty ashtrays by TST and Harker. $8-10.

On the back of these coasters are lapel pins turning them into salesmen's tags used at pottery shows. The patterns on these two are Boutonniere and Autumn Spiral. $12-15.

All of these pieces are of a lightweight ceramic body — not the normal weight associated with TST dinnerware from any era. However, they have decals used by TST: Leaf O' Gold on the goblets and Golden Day on the decanter. Values: UND.

It is not uncommon to find a TST decal or other type of decoration on shapes made by another pottery. There are several reasons why this might happen. Two or more potteries might be involved in filling a large order. There are instances where the Hall China Company would produce a line of kitchenware with a certain decal and TST would produce the dinnerware version. One pottery might produce a line with a second taking it over if the first pottery stopped making the order or closed down. Also, many of the potteries in the Ohio River Valley area used the same decal making companies. Some decals were commercial and could be used by anyone. Shown here are just a few instances of outside companies making products with treatments identical to TST.

KT&K's Victory shape casserole with TST's 601 treatment. Value: UND.

Rose Lattice 6" plate by TST (pattern 811), sugar and creamer by an unidentified pottery. Value: UND.

W. S. George's Ranchero shape with TST's Jamaica decals. Value: UND.

KT&K's Victory shape teapot with TST's 601 treatment. Value: UND.

In the late 1950s and early 1960s, TST produced a snack set made up of a welled shell plate and a Catalina teacup. They have been found in Pebbleford pink, plain white with gold trim (as shown), and from the Holly & Spruce line. More than likely other patterns will show up.

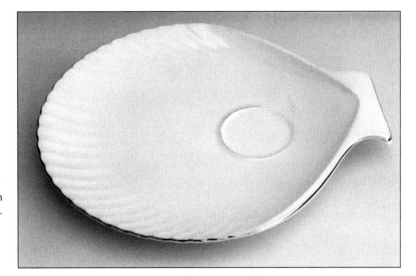

Shell snack plate in white with gold trim. $8-10.

Salad bowls were made in the early 1940s for Lu-Ray Pastels. They, along with chop plates, are often found with decals. Most of the time, they are the result of "scrap prints." It was a good way to use up older or excess decals.

Salad bowl with yellow daisies treatment. $10-12.

Demitasse set from the early 1940s. See the values section in the appendix for prices.

A special demitasse set was made in 1930 in a plain form that could be used with different dinnerware lines. Each piece was made in cylindrical form or "straight sides." This style lasted though the entire 1930s and was the basis for the original Lu-Ray Pastels demitasse set. By 1940, it was phased out in favor of a demitasse set based on the Empire shape. Both sets can be found in the Lu-Ray glazes as well as with decals. To avoid confusion between the two, collectors have adopted the name "chocolate set" for the original demitasse set.

Demitasse set from the early 1930s. See values section in the appendix for prices.

In 1976, TST offered four collector sets celebrating the nation's bicentennial. The Bicentennial Plate is very easy to find. Complete with gift box, they were made solely as a collector's item. A set was made of four Bicentennial mugs decorated with eagle, '76 flag, drum, and liberty bell decals. They had colored interiors (blue for the drum, yellow for the eagle and bell, and plain for the flag) and gold trim. A second set was made, called "Americana" sets, but without the colored interiors. The final collector's set was a six-piece set of historical plates depicting scenes from the Revolutionary War. The set consisted of one of each of the following: Surrender at Cornwallis, Betsy Ross, Washington Crossing the Delaware, Battle of Bunker Hill, Declaration of Independence, and The Spirit of '76. Of the four collector sets, the six-piece Revolutionary War set is the most difficult to find.

Bicentennial plate with box. $7-9.

Bicentennial Taylor mugs. $7-9.

Appendices
Appendix I: Decal Names and Numbers

The table that follows lists official treatment numbers used by the Taylor, Smith & Taylor Company. The only patterns listed are the ones where the name could be verified by company records or vintage advertisements. Descriptions for the many banded treatments as well as the official patterns used on Lu-Ray Pastels are also listed.

Pattern numbers were often stamped over the glaze on creamers. Once in a while the numbers can be found on sugars, oval bakers or plates. Collectors should realize the number is the proper way to identify a pattern. Retailers could name a line whatever they wanted. For example, the popular treatment 1631 was called "Scroll Border" by TST, but different carriers gave it different names. As a result, 1631 is also known as Debutante, Brown Seal, Lorraine, and Victoria. In each case, the pattern number is the same: 1631.

Once in a while a piece can be found with a full treatment number. A piece may have a handwritten code such as LOI5/1244 1/2. This would stand for: Laurel shape in the Old Ivory glaze, selection 5, pattern number 1244 1/2. For identification purposes, it is more important to be concerned with the pattern number and not the shape, glaze, and selection letters and numbers.

Patterns labeled "BT" in the table below represent banded treatments. Each treatment lists the progression of lines and bands from the rim to the verge. This listing represents what would be found on flatware and larger hollowware. Smaller pieces (saucers, cups, fruit cups, etc.) will commonly have abbreviated versions to fit the proportion of the piece. A "line" is typically thin such as simple edge trim often found on dinnerware. A "band" is thicker than a line and can vary in size. If the decoration on handles and feet of hollowware is known, it will be noted. The six treatments listed with asterisks are given in very general terms with no specifics as to size or placement of bands.

The table also lists patterns that were created for use on Lu-Ray Pastels. There is no reason why these patterns can't be found on other shapes with the same treatment numbers. The "Chatham Modern" treatments all appear on Lu-Ray Chatham Gray and are made up of a thick band encased by two lines, all of the same color.

TST used over 100 different types of gold and platinum stamp decorations alone and in conjunction with decals and underglaze treatments. The drawings represent sixty of the most common and popular of these stamps. In the treatment list below, if a treatment used one of these stamps it is either denoted by GST for gold stamp or PST for platinum stamp. For example, pattern 1922, called "Winston," uses a floral decal with GST56 or gold stamp number 56. While the treatment numbers listed are ones actually used by TST, these particular stamp numbers were not. They have been created for this book to make identification easier. Treatment descriptions starting with "ST" denote stamp treatments that do not use any decals.

If a number fails to appear in the list below, then it is because a name could not be found or an appropriate description could not be used. Many of the numbers missing in the list are of floral decal treatments. It has been decided it would not be helpful to the reader to list descriptions of the hundreds of floral decals that are so very similar to one another.

A sprig, or spray, is a decal. Some treatments are made up of different sizes and styles of sprigs. In the treatment descriptions, if the number of sprigs is known, it is noted. For example, 916 is Paramount Rose with two sprigs, or "2s," whereas 917 has one sprig or "1s."

ST1

ST2

ST3

ST4

ST5

ST6

ST7

ST8

ST9

ST10

ST11

ST12

ST13

ST14

ST15

ST16

ST17

ST18

ST19

ST20

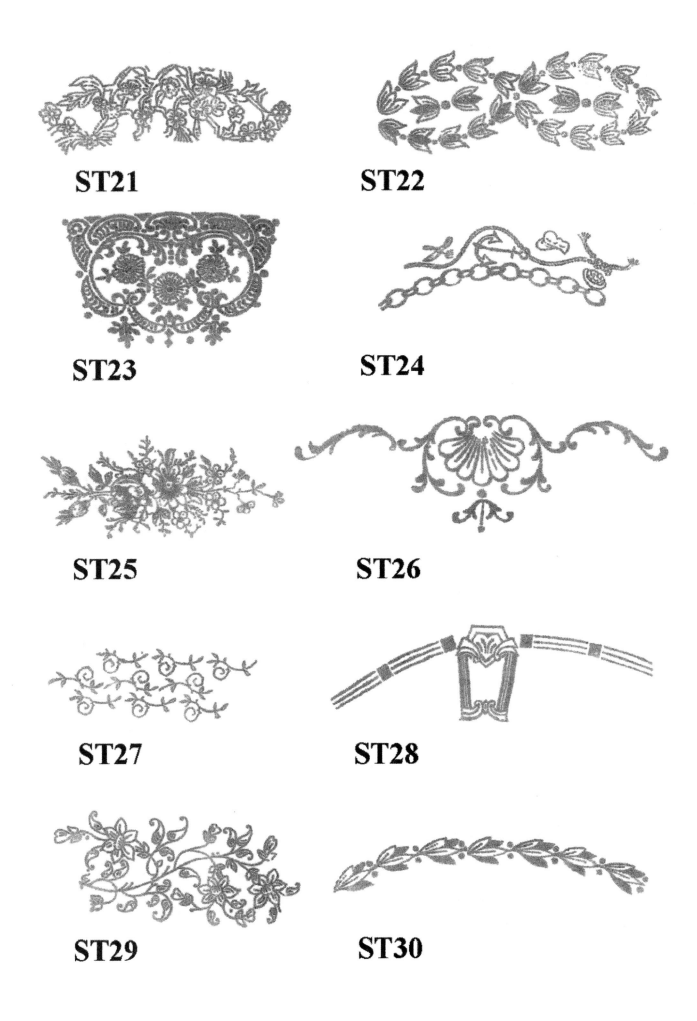

ST21

ST22

ST23

ST24

ST25

ST26

ST27

ST28

ST29

ST30

ST31

ST32

ST33

ST34

ST35

ST36

ST37

ST38

ST39

ST40

ST41

ST42

ST43

ST44

ST45

ST46

ST47

ST48

ST49

ST50

ST51

ST52

ST53

ST54

ST55

ST56

ST57

ST58

ST59

ST60

Treatment	Name and/or Description	Treatment	Name and/or Description
4	BT: white band with black lines	120	BT: matte silver verge line on Paramount shape
5	BT: white band with red lines		
6	BT: platinum drop band	122	BT: gold trim
7	BT: yellow drop band	123	BT: blue verge line
8	BT: rose drop band	126	Red Hollyhock, green edge line
9	BT: blue drop band	128	Hollyhock, green edge line
15	BT: gold drop band, gold fine line	138	Coral Morning Glory, green edge line
20	BT: turquoise drop band, black line	140	Gold Tulip, gray edge line
21	BT: green drop band, black line	143	BT: platinum verge band
27	BT: black drop band and line	144	Gold Tulip, gray verge band
28	BT: royal blue drop band and line	146	Crab Apple
29	BT: platinum trim	148	BT: black verge line
33	BT: gold trim and gold embossing on Avona shape	149	BT: green band and verge line
		150	BT: green band and black fine line
35	BT: platinum trim and platinum embossing on Avona shape	151	BT: green band and black verge line
		152	BT: coral band and black verge line
37	Hollyhock, green verge line	153	BT: coral band and black fine line
38	Red Hollyhock, Ivory two-tone, green verge line	154	BT: platinum band and coral fine line
		155	BT: royal blue verge line
39	"Colored glaze with coral handles only"	164	Crab Apple, black edge line
40	"Colored glaze with green handles only"	166	Red Hollyhock, platinum edge band
41	"Colored glaze with royal blue handles only"	171	BT: gold edge band
42	"Colored glaze with platinum handles only"	172	BT: gold edge and body line
43	"Colored glaze with yellow handles only"	173	BT: platinum edge and black fine line
44	"Colored glaze with gold handles only"	175	Crab Apple, green edge line
52	BT: green edge band, gold verge on Paramount Ivory two-tone	177	Nasturtium, green connect line
		181	BT: green edge and body line
56	Red Hollyhock, green verge line	182	BT: green band and black fine lines
63	BT: gold edge band and verge line	188	BT: green verge line only
64	Spring Flowers, 2s, green trim	190	Spring Flowers, green connecting line
69	BT: platinum verge line	197	BT: gold edge band
70	BT: green verge line	208	Tudor Rose, green edge line
71	BT: coral verge line	209	Bluet, platinum trim, green verge line
72	BT: platinum edge and foot lines	211	Arbutus, platinum trim, green verge line
73	BT: green edge line, green handles and knobs	215	BT: royal blue edge and fine line
77	Blue Bird, 3s, blue edge line	216	Nasturtium, 3s, green edge line
83	BT: coral band encased by two black lines	220	Bluet, pink two-tone, platinum edge and verge lines
85	BT: green band and drop line		
95	BT: green edge and verge lines	221	Arbutus, pink two-tone, platinum edge and verge lines
104	BT: blue edge and verge lines		
109	BT: platinum edge and verge lines	235	French Rose, gray edge line
110	BT: blue band encased by two black lines	237	Pansy, 4s, platinum trim
		244	Bluet, 1s, platinum trim
111	BT: green band encased by two black lines	245	Bluet, 1s, platinum edge and verge lines
112	BT: same as 111 with only one line towards verge	246	Arbutus, 1s, platinum trim
		249	BT: three platinum lines
114	Spring Flowers, 1s, green trim	250	BT: gold edge band, black line
116	BT: gold band, black fine line	254	BT: green band
119	BT: matte silver band	256	BT: platinum band

Treatment	Name and/or Description
259	French Rose
261	Arbutus, green two-tone, green verge line, silver trim
262	Nasturtium, 2s, green edge line
263	Crab Apple, 2s, black edge line
266	BT: green fine edge line, platinum line
268	Pansy, 3s, platinum trim
270	BT: green edge line, orange body line
271	Nasturtium, 1s, green edge line
274	Pansy, 2s, platinum trim
277	Spring Flowers, 1s, gold connecting line
297	Nasturtium, 2s, green edge line
280	Arbutus, 1s, green edge line
284	BT: "Gold Band" gold edge and verge lines
301	BT: royal blue edge and fine lines
302	BT: gold edge and fine lines
303	BT: gold edge and body lines
308	Spring Flowers, 4s, platinum trim
309	Arbutus, green edge line
312	Garden
317	BT: gold edge band and body line
318	Bluet, 1s, green edge line
320	Orchid, 3s, platinum trim
321	Orchid, 2s, platinum trim
322	Orchid, 1s, platinum trim
330	Crab Apple, 3s, silver edge line
331	Hollyhock, platinum edge line
335	Silver Rose, 3s, platinum trim
336	Silver Rose, 1s, platinum trim
337	Silver Rose, 2s, platinum trim
345	Garden, 2s, platinum trim
346	Garden, 2s, green edge line
347	Thistle, platinum trim, black drop line
355	Nasturtium, no line
358	BT: gold edge and body lines
361	Bluet, 1s, green two-tone, green edge, and verge lines
363	Crab Apple, 1s, green connect line
366	Yellow Rose, 3s, red edge line
369	Garden, 2s, green two-tone, green verge line
370	Thistle, platinum trim
372	BT: thick gold edge band
378	Thistle, no trim, Platinum handles
380	Thistle, platinum trim, violet drop line
382	BT: gold edge and body lines
384	BT: platinum band and body line
386	BT: gold edge band
391	Morning Glories (deco style), 2s, platinum trim
397	Daisies, 3s, green edge line
411	BT: green edge line and red line on flange
412	Heathertone (gold trim)
414	Daisies, 1s, green edge line
417	BT: green band and verge line
421	Daisies, 2s, green edge line
424	Heathertone (platinum trim)
425	BT: gold edge and fine line
450	Apple Blossoms, 2s, platinum trim, brown verge
455	Arbutus, 1s, platinum trim, pink verge line
459	Daisies, platinum trim
470	BT: royal blue band and fine line
477	Daisies, 1s, platinum trim
481	BT: thick gold edge and gold band verge
486	Daisies, 3s, platinum trim
492	BT: green edge line only
494	Daisies, 2s, platinum trim
499	BT: green edge and verge fine lines
501	BT: royal blue edge and verge fine lines
503	Blue Willow (Decal)
507	Bird of Paradise
509	Fountain
512	BT: gold fan line (for Avona shape)
524	BT: drop gold band
525	BT: green edge line and stroke on handles
529	Wisteria, green drop band, platinum trim
532	Serenade, no trim
544	BT: platinum edge and red verge lines
545	Italian Rose, blue edge line
546	BT: three platinum lines, three gray lines — varying widths
547	Jonquil, 2s, platinum trim
548	Jonquil
549	Jonquil, 1s, platinum trim, two yellow lines
551	BT: gold edge and royal blue body lines
555	BT: six platinum lines — varying widths, fine lines on handles
556	BT: same as 546 with solid platinum foot on hollowware
558	BT: platinum edge line, gray band, three pink lines
559	BT: platinum edge line, green band, three gray lines
560	Blue Vase, 1s, platinum trim
563	English Cottage, 1s, platinum trim
564	Yellow Ships, 3s, platinum trim
565	Green Wheel, platinum trim and green band
566	Blue Wheel, platinum trim and blue band

Treatment	Name and/or Description
576	Orange Wheel, platinum trim and red band
577	Grey Wheel, platinum trim and gray band
591	Black Laurel, platinum trim
592	Blue Laurel, platinum trim
593	Red Laurel, platinum trim
596	Fruit Basket, red band and brown line
599	BT: green band, platinum line
600	BT: six coin gold lines — varying widths, solid handles, and foot
601	BT: "Sterling" — six platinum lines — varying widths, solid handles, and foot
605	BT: "Rainbow" — platinum edge line, four color lines, platinum verge line
606	BT: platinum edge line, five green lines, platinum verge line
608	BT: platinum edge line, yellow line, red band, yellow line, platinum verge line
609	BT: platinum edge line, yellow line, brown band, yellow line, platinum verge line
613	Wisteria, platinum trim
615	Blue Vase, 1s, yellow line
617	BT: blue band, platinum band, blue line, platinum line, blue fine line, platinum fine line
618	BT: platinum edge line, red band, two platinum bands, red band, platinum verge line
619	BT: platinum edge line, red line, three platinum lines, yellow band
620	BT: platinum edge line, platinum band, dark gray band, light gray band, platinum band
626	BT: platinum edge and flange lines
628	Italian Rose, green edge line
629	Spring Flowers, 1s, platinum trim
641	Italian Rose, blue edge line
643	Holdfast Decal
644	Silhouette (Tavern)
646	Wheaties Decal
653	BT: gold band edge
654	BT: three coin gold lines
655	Jonquil, 1s, platinum trim
664	Fruit Basket, platinum trim
675	Morning Glories (deco style), 3s, platinum trim
684	ST: PST2, no trim
689	Miami, black edge, green band, yellow line
690	BT: bright gold band edge and verge line
698	ST: gold border stamp
702	BT: platinum edge band
704	Green Ribbon, platinum trim
707	ST: GST37 with gold trim

Treatment	Name and/or Description
718	Green Flower Pot, black edge, green band, yellow line
719	Coral Flower Pot, black edge, red band, yellow line
720	Red Ships, 3s, platinum trim
722	BT: platinum edge and foot lines, black and red handles
723	Green Flower Pot, green edge line
728	BT: platinum edge line, blue band, platinum line, blue band, platinum line, blue line, platinum line
730	BT: green band, gray band, green line, gray line, green fine line, gray fine line
731	BT: red band, gray band, red line, gray line, red fine line, gray fine line
732	BT: blue shaded flange
733	BT: black shaded flange
734	BT: brown shaded flange
735	BT: gold edge line, red band, gold line, red band, gold line, red band, gold line
736	BT: platinum edge line, black band, platinum line, black band, platinum line, black band, platinum line
737	BT: platinum edge line, blue band, platinum line, violet band, platinum line, gray band, platinum line
739	BT: platinum panels (for Vogue shape)
740	ST: gold center stamp and border
741	ST: gold center stamp and border
743	BT: red edge and foot lines, black and red handles
747	ST: GST43 and gold line
748	ST: GST37 and center stamp with gold trim
751	ST: GST31 with gold trim
757	BT: gold edge, thick maroon band, gold band, gold line, gold verge line
758	BT: gold edge, thick green band, gold band, gold line, gold verge line
759	ST: "Vogue" PST40 with platinum trim
762	ST: gold border stamp
769	Leaves, green trim
772	Red Plaid
777	Coral Flower Pot, orange trim
779	BT: red drop line, red drop foot line, red and black handles
784	Pink Swedish Modern, platinum trim
786	Blue Plaid
787	Green Plaid
788	Black Plaid
789	Yellow Plaid

Treatment	Name and/or Description	Treatment	Name and/or Description
790	ST: GST32 with gold trim	936	Pink Swedish Modern, 6s and center, platinum trim and pink verge line
792	ST: Gold border stamp with gold trim	939	BT: gold edge line, green band, two gold lines, gold verge line
794	ST: PST37 with platinum trim		
795	Yellow Swedish Modern, platinum trim	955	BT: platinum edge band, black verge
796	Blue Swedish Modern, platinum trim	956	BT: yellow edge line, green line, green band, four yellow lines, green line, yellow verge line
801	ST: GST19 with green dapple edge		
804	ST: PST43 with platinum trim		
805	ST: PST32 with platinum trim	957	BT: platinum edge line, yellow band, four platinum lines, yellow band, platinum line, yellow line, platinum line
811	Rose Lattice, gold verge line		
812	ST: PST18 with platinum trim		
813	ST: PST42 with platinum trim		
820	Wild Poppy, 1s, red edge line	958	BT: seven black, yellow and green lines*
821	Cross Stitch Cottage and border, platinum trim	959	BT: five yellow and gold lines and bands*
		960	BT: four brown and yellow lines and band*
823	BT: platinum edge line, brown band, yellow band, brown band, yellow band	963	BT: platinum edge line, two platinum lines, three fine platinum lines
824	BT: platinum edge line, green band, gray band, green band, gray band	964	BT: four platinum, black and red lines and bands*
825	Golden Pinwheel (HP gold embossing on Vogue shape)	965	BT: nine platinum and green lines and bands*
		975	ST: eight small gold leaf stamps, gold trim
829	Wild Poppy, 2s, red edge line	976	BT: gold edge thick band, gold fine line, gold band
835	ST: PST21 with platinum trim		
840	Fuji (Hall China's name for the decal), black edge line	997	BT: platinum edge band and verge lines, solid platinum foot
841	BT: black trim, no decal	998	BT: gold edge band and black verge line, solid gold foot
842	ST: GST42 with gold trim		
843	ST: GST52 with gold trim	1004	Delphian Rose
844	ST: GST33 with gold trim	1015	Blue Floral Spray, 1s, blue verge line
847	Blue Urn, platinum trim	1023	Yellow Daisies, yellow verge line
873	Blue Garland, UG	1025	BT: gold edge band, gold verge band, four gold fine lines
875	Pink Garland, UG		
877	Leaves, 10s, green trim	1026	BT: four platinum, black and green lines and bands*
881	Blue Bouquet, UG		
893	Dogwood, UG	1029	BT: platinum drop band and verge line
905	ST: PST19 with platinum trim	1039	BT: red verge band
911	ST: GST33 with gold trim	1040	BT: brown verge band
916	Paramount Rose, 2s, platinum trim	1041	BT: green verge band
917	Paramount Rose, 1s, platinum trim	1109	Black Checker
921	Blue Floral Spray, 1s, platinum trim, green verge	1110	Green Checker
		1113	Bouquet, GST43 and gold trim
922	Blue Floral Spray, 1s, platinum trim	1115	ST: "Lexington" PST16 with platinum trim
922	Blue Floral Spray, platinum trim and green drop band	1116	ST: GST16 with gold trim
		1117	UG: hand-painted forget-me-nots
929	ST: GST42 with gold edge line	1128	BT: wide platinum drop band, black verge
933	ST: platinum center stamp and trim	1134	Nestlé's, maroon edge line
934	ST: wide platinum band with incrusted laurel stamp and platinum verge line	1135	Popeye, no trim
		1136	ST: GST19 with gold trim
935	ST: wide gold band with incrusted laurel stamp and black verge line	1137	Popeye, no trim, GST34
		1139	BT: gold edge line, gold line, gold fine line

1142   BT: same as 1139 with lines close together at the rim

1151   Cross Stitch Rose, side spray, GST48 with gold trim

1153   UG: Black Maple Leaf

1154   UG: Green Maple Leaf

1155   UG: Green Tulip, gold trim

1156   Cross Stitch flower pots, 6s along rim, platinum trim

1157   UG: Pink Rose (center), gold edge and verge lines

1158   Cross Stitch Cottage, 1s, platinum trim

1162   Yellow Daisies, gold trim

1163   ST: PST1, platinum edge and verge lines

1165   Cross Stitch Rose, platinum trim

1169   ST: PST28 with platinum edge and verge lines

1177   Green Wheat, platinum trim, black verge line

1178   Modern Border (coral tone), platinum trim

1179   Modern Border (green tone), platinum trim

1180   Blue Wheat, platinum trim, black verge line

1183   Green Harp

1184   Brown Harp

1190   Bouquet, GST12 with gold trim

1191   Dresden Rose, GST45 with gold trim

1192   Dresden Rose, GST56 with gold trim

1194   Wild Poppy, gold trim

1198   Popeye, GST36

1199   Popeye, Blue Stamp-36

1200   BT: red drop band

1201   BT: blue drop band

1202   BT: green drop band

1203   Popeye, Blue Stamp-24

1211   Bouquet. GST56 with gold trim

1212   Lace Needlepoint (center) platinum trim

1213   Lace Needlepoint (center) GST48, gold trim

1214   Autumn Leaves, platinum, red and brown lines

1215   Autumn Leaves, red edge line

1218   Autumn Leaves, platinum trim

1223   Blue Gingham Plaid, platinum trim

1222   Yellow Daisies, GST56, gold trim

1225   Coral Gingham Plaid, platinum trim

1227   Green Flower Basket, platinum and green lines

1228   Green Flower Basket, platinum, green and gray lines

1229   Melba, platinum trim

1230   Melba, platinum, blue and orange lines

1233   Blue Delphinium, platinum trim

1234   Lace Needlepoint (center) GST54, gold trim

1236   Lace Needlepoint (border and center), gold trim

1247   BT: same as 1139, but in red

1248   BT: same as 1139, but in green

1249   White Flowers (green tone), platinum trim, green band, gray band

1250   White Flowers (green tone), green, black and platinum lines

1251   White Flowers (green tone), platinum trim

1253   Cross Stitch Rose (border and center), platinum trim

1254   Red Checker

1264   Yellow Daisies, PST30, platinum trim

1266   Gold Harp

1267   White Flowers (coral tone), coral, gray and platinum lines

1268   White Flowers (coral tone), coral band, gray and platinum lines

1269   Green Flower Basket, platinum trim, green verge

1270   BT: gold edge band, three black lines

1271   Cross Stitch Rose (side), GST30, gold trim

1273   Red Wheat, platinum trim

1274   ST: PST15, platinum trim

1275   ST: GST15, gold trim

1277   Lace Needlepoint (center), green edge line

1278   ST: PST43, platinum trim

1279   Modern Border (blue tone), platinum trim

1282   ST: GST15 with gold verge stamp

1292   Melba, platinum and blue lines

1295   ST: GST14 with gold trim

1297   Green Ribbon, platinum trim

1299   Red Wheat, platinum trim, black verge

1301   BT: platinum band, blue verge line and accents on tops of handles, Empire shape only

1302   BT: same as 1301 in yellow

1303   BT: same as 1301 in green

1304   Gold Monogram

1305   BT: same as 1301 in black

1306   Autumn Leaves, red edge and brown fine line

1307   ST: GST25 with gold trim

1308   ST: GST11 with gold trim

1309   White Flowers (green tone), platinum trim, platinum verge stamp

1316   Ships

1327   BT: three red lines

1328   BT: three royal blue lines

1329   BT: three green lines

1330   BT: same as 1301 in red

1331   Tulip Cluster, platinum trim

Treatment	Name and/or Description		Treatment	Name and/or Description
1332	ST: TT ivory wash vellum on flange, GST17, gold trim and verge lines, blue band at edge		1407	Blue Bell, 1s, platinum trim
1333	ST: same as 1332 in green		1408	Briar Rose, 2s, platinum trim
1334	ST: same as 1332 in red		1409	Briar Rose, 1s, platinum trim
1335	UG: dark blue underglaze panels with gold over stamp		1422	Fruit and Flowers, platinum trim
1336	UG: same as 1335 in pink		1423	Iris, 1s, platinum trim
1338	White Flowers (green tone) platinum trim, gray line		1424	Gloria, 4s, platinum trim
			1425	Gloria, 2s, platinum trim
1339	BT: blue band edge with blue accents on tops of handles, Empire shape only		1426	Gloria, 1s, platinum trim
			1429	Sylvia, 2s, platinum trim
1340	Platinum Monogram		1430	Sylvia, 1s, platinum trim
1341	BT: same as 1339 in red with platinum verge line		1431	What Not, platinum trim
			1432	Pansy, 4s, platinum trim
1342	Symphony		1433	Umbrella, platinum trim
1344	Pansy (flowerpot) with gold edge line		1436	Flower Cart, 2s, red edge line
1349	Hunt Scene, black edge and red fine lines		1437	Flower Cart, 2s, platinum trim
1351	Napoli, 2s, green drop line		1440	Vegetable Basket, 1s, platinum trim
1352	Rio Rita		1441	Clairmont, gold edge line
1353	Mayflower		1442	Forget-me-not, 1s, platinum trim
1354	BT: bright gold edge band		1444	Ivy Border
1356	Rose Marie, gold trim		1445	Duchess, platinum beads with encasing lines, Plymouth shape
1357	UG: Dutch Windmill, pink			
1358	UG: Dutch Windmill, blue		1446	same as 1445 in gold
1359	UG: Dutch Windmill, green		1447	same as 1445 with blue and red encasing lines
1360	UG: Dutch Windmill, black		1448	BT: two green lines
1363	Tulip Time, 2s, blue drop line		1449	BT: platinum edge, red line, black line
1364	Modern Morning Glory, green edge and red fine line		1450	BT: platinum edge and red lines
			1451	BT: two platinum lines
1365	Calla Lily, green drop and edge lines		1455	Briar Rose, 2s, platinum trim
1366	Modern Morning Glory, platinum edge		1456	Briar Rose, 1s, platinum trim
1367	Calla Lily, gold trim		1457	Hyde Park Tulips, platinum trim
1368	BT: blue, red, and green lines		1458	Orchid, 1s, platinum trim
1369	Pansy (flowerpot) gold trim and green fine line		1459	BT: same as 963 with platinum lines
			1460	Tulip Time, 1s, blue drop line
1370	Pansy (flowerpot) green drop line		1463	Napoli, 1s, green drop line
1371	Modern Morning Glory, platinum trim		1464	Napoli, 1s, green drop line
1373	Tulip Time, red drop line		1466	What Not, blue trim
1377	Melody, gold trim		1469	Forget-me-not, 1s, blue edge line
1378	Vegetable Kingdom, blue trim		1471	BT: platinum edge line only
1379	Chicken Fight, red drop line		1472	BT: gold edge line only
1395	BT: red edge band, yellow line, three blue lines		1474	Dresden Rose, PST44
			1475	Dresden Rose, ivory two-tone with PST44
1396	Wheat, 1s, gold trim		1476	Dresden Rose, ivory two-tone with PST44 and platinum trim
1398	Holland Mills (Dutch Vista) red trim			
1399	Strawberry		1477	White Flowers (coral tone), platinum trim
1400	Stage Coach, UG in gold		1478	White Flowers (green tone), platinum trim
1401	BT: same as 1339 in green		1479	Miami, platinum edge and green band
1405	ST: GST1 with gold trim		1480	Cottage, 2s, platinum trim
1406	Blue Bell, 2s, platinum trim		1481	Cottage, 1s, platinum trim
			1484	Chelsea, Acacia, 4s, gold trim
			1485	BT: gold coin edge line and band

Treatment	Name and/or Description
1486	ST: GST19 and gold trim
1502	Water Lily, green edge line
1503	Water Lily, platinum trim
1505	Fifth Avenue, blue trim
1506	Fifth Avenue, platinum trim
1507	Daffodil, gold trim
1508	Daffodil, green trim
1509	BT: Hostess, platinum verge line and platinum lines
1510	Mexican Fantasy, red trim
1511	Mexican Fantasy (Adobe), blue trim
1512	Dwarf Tulip, 3s, platinum trim
1513	Barberry, red trim
1514	Barberry, gold trim
1516	Home Spun Tulip, green trim
1517	Home Spun Tulip, gold trim
1518	Mexican Fantasy (Adobe), red trim
1519	Clairmont, three gold lines
1523	Home Spun Tulip, two-tone, gold trim, green verge
1526	Clairmont, ivory two-tone, gold verge line
1529	Water Lily, ivory two-tone, gold edge and verge lines
1531	Orchid, 1s, gold trim
1532	Dresden Rose
1533	Dresden Rose, GST56, gold edge line and blue band
1535	Dwarf Tulip, 3s, gold trim
1537	Dwarf Tulip, 1s, no trim
1538	Hyde Park Tulips, red trim
1539	Gloria, 2s, two-tone, gold edge and verge lines
1540	BT: gold edge line, blue band, gold line
1541	ST: double GST44 on either side of blue band, ivory two-tone body, gold edge and verge lines
1543	Pansy (flowerpot) GST51 with gold trim, maroon band
1545	Bouquet, GST51 with gold trim, maroon band
1546	BT: thick gold edge band, black verge line
1554	Italian Flora, yellow band
1555	Italian Flora, green band
1556	Yellow Deco Flowers, yellow band
1557	Yellow Deco Flowers, lavender band
1558	Orange Deco Wreath, pink band
1559	Orange Deco Wreath, yellow band
1562	ST: gold border ribbon stamp and gold trim
1565	Pink Swedish Modern, no trim
1566	Pink Swedish Modern, pink band
1571	BT: gold band and verge lines
1572	Peasant, blue band
1573	LRT: yellow deco flowers, Lu-Ray blue, no trim
1574	LRT: orange deco wreath, Lu-Ray yellow, no trim
1575	LRT: Italian Flora, Lu-Ray yellow, no trim
1576	LRT: five brown lines on Lu-Ray yellow
1577	LRT: five maroon lines on Ly-Ray pink
1578	LRT: Peasant on Lu-Ray yellow, no trim
1579	LRT: Fifth Avenue on Lu-Ray blue, no trim
1580	LRT: five blue lines on Lu-Ray blue
1581	LRT: Water Lily on Lu-Ray green, no trim
1582	Lace Needlepoint, gold edge line
1583	LRT: Water Lily on Lu-Ray yellow, green band
1584	LRT: Fifth Avenue on Lu-Ray blue, blue band
1585	LRT: Italian Flora, Lu-Ray yellow, green band
1586	LRT: Peasant, Lu-Ray yellow, brown band
1587	LRT: five gray lines on Lu-Ray green
1588	LRT: three black lines on Lu-Ray green
1589	LRT: two maroon edge lines and maroon band on verge on Lu-Ray pink
1590	LRT: two brown edge lines and brown band on verge on Lu-Ray yellow
1591	LRT: two yellow edge lines and yellow band on verge on Lu-Ray yellow
1592	LRT: two blue edge lines and gray band on verge on Lu-Ray blue
1593	LRT: two green edge lines and green band on verge on Lu-Ray green
1594	LRT: yellow flange on Lu-Ray yellow
1598	Dresden Rose, GST10
1599	Dresden Rose, red band with gold encasing lines
1601	BT: three fine platinum lines towards verge, platinum verge band, no edge line
1602	Myrna, yellow band
1604	Myrna, pink band
1605	Myrna, green band
1606	BT: green band
1607	BT: yellow band
1608	BT: lavender band
1609	BT: pink band
1610	ST: double GST44 on either side of blue band, gold edge and verge lines
1611	Dresden Rose, GST44 and two gold lines
1613	BT: four platinum lines
1614	Orange Deco Wreath, yellow flange
1615	Italian Flora, green flange
1616	Yellow Deco Flowers, lavender flange

Treatment	Name and/or Description
1617	Italian Flora, yellow flange
1618	Pink Swedish Modern, pink flange
1619	ST: GST41 with red band
1620	BT: three red lines on flange
1621	ST: GST46 with red flange
1622	Italian Flora, blue band
1623	Italian Flora, pink band
1627	Wheat, gold band
1630	Elaine, Mildred, gold trim
1631	Debutante, Brown Seal, Scroll Border, Lorraine, Victoria, gold trim
1633	Peasant Rose, Floral Bouquet, no trim
1632	LRT: white flower on Lu-Ray pink
1634	Peasant Rose, red trim
1635	Peasant Rose, green trim
1639	Blue Spiral Rose, heavy blue edge
1641	Yellow Spiral Rose, heavy yellow edge
1643	Pink Peasant Spray, platinum trim
1644	Pink Peasant Spray, pink edge line
1645	Green Peasant Spray, platinum trim
1646	Green Peasant Spray, green edge line
1648	Dresden Rose, red band between two gold lines
1649	Pine Cone, gold trim
1651	Myrna, GST10
1652	Pine Cone, green trim
1653	Moss Rose, Sherwood, gold trim
1655	BT: gold edge and verge lines, red flange, GST10
1656	BT: gold edge and verge lines, yellow flange, GST10
1657	BT: gold edge and verge lines, green flange, GST10
1658	BT: gold edge and verge lines, blue flange, GST10
1659	Myrna, ruby band encased by two gold lines
1660	Myrna, yellow band encased by two gold lines
1661	Myrna, green band encased by two gold lines
1662	Myrna, blue band encased by two gold lines
1668	LRT: red edge and verge lines on Lu-Ray yellow
1669	LRT: green edge and verge lines on Lu-Ray yellow
1671	Briar Rose, 1s, dark brown and light brown bands
1673	ST: GST3 with gold trim
1674	Myrna, red band
1676	ST: GST46 with gold trim, red flange
1679	LRT: red edge and verge, solid red handles, Lu-Ray yellow
1680	Myrna, blue band
1681	Dresden Rose, blue band between two gold lines
1682	Dresden Rose, same as 1681
1684	Bouquet, GST56 with gold edge and verge lines
1686	Dresden Rose, GST53 with gold edge and verge lines on red flange
1688	Dresden Rose, GST53 with gold edge and verge lines on green flange
1687	Dresden Rose, GST53 with gold edge and verge lines on yellow flange
1690	Dresden Rose, GST20 with gold edge and verge lines
1692	Dresden Rose, PST20 with platinum edge and verge lines
1693	BT: coin gold trim and fans on the Avona shape
1694	BT: bright gold trim and fans on the Avona shape
1695	BT: platinum trim and fans on the Avona shape
1697	Forget-me-not
1698	Dresden Rose, Royal Gold, GST41 with gold edge and verge lines
1699	ST: GST41 with gold edge and verge lines
1700	LRT: ruby red edge and verge lines on Lu-Ray yellow
1701	LRT: yellow edge and verge lines on Lu-Ray blue
1702	LRT: green edge and verge lines on Lu-Ray pink
1703	LRT: pink edge and verge lines on Lu-Ray green
1704	Dresden Rose, same as 1698
1706	Dresden Rose, GS52 and gold trim
1707	Myrna, GST25 and gold trim
1711	Dresden Rose, GST10 and gold trim
1712	Pansy, 4s, gold dapple
1713	Dresden Rose, bright gold dapple
1716	Pansy, 4s, platinum dapple
1717	Dresden Rose, gold ribbon stamp and gold trim
1718	same as 1236
1720	Bouquet, GST56 with gold trim
1721	Dresden Rose, GST56 with gold trim

Treatment	Name and/or Description
1722	Bouquet, GST12 with gold trim
1723	Dresden Rose, yellow band and gold encasing lines
1724	Dresden Rose, green band and gold encasing lines
1725	Dresden Rose with clover decal border
1726	Dresden Rose with green decal border
1727	Leaves, 16s, gold trim
1728	Lace Needlepoint, GS, gold trim
1729	Dresden Rose, five platinum lines
1732	Dresden Rose, GST25 with gold trim
1734	Yellow Daisies, GST25 with gold trim
1735	Lace Needlepoint, GST25 with gold trim
1737	Water Lily, GST25 with gold trim
1739	Yellow Daisies, GST52 with gold trim
1740	Dresden Rose, gold trim and fans and gold verge line (Avona shape)
1745	Dresden Rose, five coin gold lines
1748	Fruit and Flowers, GST52 with gold trim
1764	Bouquet, GST12, no trim
1770	BT: red edge line and three red lines
1771	Bouquet, GST52 and gold trim
1772	ST: GST8 with gold verge and edge lines
1773	ST: GST42, no trim
1774	ST: GST11 with gold trim on red flange
1775	ST: GST11 with gold trim on yellow flange
1799	Leaves, platinum edge line
1780	Moss Rose
1781	Carnation, ivory two-tone, matte gold edge and verge lines
1782	Carnation, gold trim
1784	Elite
1785	Mayfair, (same as 1631), two-tone and two gold matte lines
1786	Mayfair
1789	Cabbage Rose, two-tone with matte gold lines
1790	Cabbage Rose, gold trim
1793	ST: GST9 on ivory two-tone body with gold matte lines.
1794	ST: GST9 with gold trim
1795	ST: GST22 with gold trim
1797	Sheridan (same as Scroll Border but on an ivory two-tone body)
1798	ST: GST8, no trim
1799	Danbury, ivory two-tone, two matte lines
1802	ST: "Daphne" or "Gold Laurel" GST8 on ivory two-tone body with gold matte lines
1083	ST: GST22 on ivory two-tone body with gold matte lines
1804	Myrna, two-tone, gold edge and verge lines, GST22
1805	ST: "Ramona" GST3 on ivory two-tone body with gold matte lines
1806	ST: GST23 on ivory two-tone body with gold matte lines
1807	ST: GST3 with gold trim
1808	Dresden Rose, blue band between two gold lines
1811	BT: same as 782, solid platinum foot and handles
1812	Florette, Winston, ivory two-tone body with two gold lines
1822	Bouquet, GST25 and gold trim
1823	Green Briar, gold trim
1824	Mayfair, matte gold lines
1825	ST: PST58 with platinum lines
1826	Moss Rose, 1s, gold trim
1829	Dresden Rose, ST35 and blue band
1830	Dresden Rose, ST35 and salmon band
1831	Florette, Winston, two-tone ivory body with gold lines
1832	Cabbage Rose, salmon and gray bands
1834	Lace Needlepoint, GST56 on the verge
1835	Green Flower Basket, platinum edge and three bands: platinum, green, platinum
1836	BT: six blue and platinum bands and lines
1837	Bouquet, GST52, no trim
1838	Bouquet, GST25, no trim
1840	Cabbage Rose, gold trim and blue verge line
1841	BT: "Comstock" two-tone ivory body with matte gold edge band, black drop fine line and black verge
1842	ST: "Silver Laurel" PST8, platinum edge and blue band
1843	ST: PST8, platinum edge and salmon band
1844	ST: GST35, gold edge and salmon band
1845	ST: GST35, gold edge and blue band
1846	ST: gold stripe stamp, gold edge and red band
1847	ST: gold stripe stamp, gold edge and blue band
1848	Dresden Rose, ST56, gold edge and red band
1849	Bouquet, GST52 and gold trim
1850	ST: GST17 on ivory two-tone with blue band and gold matte lines
1851	ST: GST17 on ivory two-tone with red band and gold matte lines
1852	Dresden Rose, GST42 with gold edge and blue band

Treatment	Name and/or Description
1853	Dresden Rose, GST42 with gold edge and salmon band
1854	Bouquet, GST42 with gold edge and salmon band
1855	Bouquet, GST42 with gold edge and blue band
1856	Bouquet, GST56 with gold edge and salmon band
1857	Bouquet, GST56 with gold edge and blue band
1858	Dresden Rose, GST23 with gold trim
1860	Rosalie, two-tone ivory, blue edge and verge lines
1861	Rosalie, gold trim
1862	Chattily, two-tone ivory, green edge and verge lines
1863	Chattily, gold trim
1867	BT: four platinum lines
1868	Cabbage Rose, GST 9 and gold trim
1869	Bouquet, GST9 and gold trim
1872	BT: Platinum edge band and verge line
1874	ST: PST45 with platinum edge and verge lines
1876	ST: PST8 with platinum edge and verge lines
1877	ST: PST22 with platinum edge and verge lines
1878	ST: PST3 with platinum edge and verge lines
1879	ST: platinum scroll stamp with platinum edge and verge lines
1880	Harvest (for Quaker Oats)
1881	Acacia, ivory two-tone body with gold matte lines
1882	Blue Wheat, ivory two-tone with blue edge and verge lines
1884	Dresden Rose with border decal and gold matte lines
1887	Cabbage Rose, GST14, no trim
1888	Dresden Rose, GST50 and gold trim
1889	Bouquet, GST9 and gold trim
1890	Cabbage Rose, GST14 and gold trim
1892	ST: PST22 and platinum lines
1897	Bouquet, GST52 and gold trim
1899	Leaves, platinum trim
1904	Dresden Rose, red band between two gold lines
1905	Napoli, 2s, red drop line
1906	Umbrella, platinum edge line
1907	Dresden Rose, same as 1599 but on ivory two-tone
1908	Dresden Rose, same as 1681 but on ivory two-tone
1911	Cabbage Rose, GST52 and gold trim
1912	BT: maroon band between two gold lines
1913	Florette, Winston, gold edge line
1914	Florette, Winston, GST9 and gold trim
1915	Blue Leaf Rose, gold edge
1917	Moss Rose, 1s, green line
1920	Pink and Yellow Rose Spray (Rose Cluster), platinum trim
1922	Winston, Florette, GST56 and gold trim
1923	Pink and Yellow Rose Spray (Rose Cluster), GST25 and gold trim
1924	ST: PST25
1925	Strawberry, GST9, no trim (a.k.a. pattern 1925 1/2)
1926	Cabbage Rose, GST56 on the verge
1927	Cabbage Rose, GST41, no trim
1929	Dresden Rose , GST52 and gold trim
1931	Dresden Rose, Sydney, GST3 and gold trim
1934	Blue Leaf Rose, GST52 and gold trim
1935	Cabbage Rose, red band and two gold lines
1936	Cabbage Rose, blue band and two gold lines
1937	Blue Leaf Rose, GST49, blue band and gold trim
1938	Blue Leaf Rose, GST49, salmon band and gold trim
1939	Cabbage Rose, three platinum bands in style of top "601" bands
1940	Cabbage Rose, three gold bands in style of top "600" bands
1941	Cabbage Rose, GST32 with gold lines
1942	Blue Leaf Rose, GST8 with gold lines
1943	Clairmont with GST44 (same decal used in 1799)
1944	Cabbage Rose, GST49 on the verge
1947	Pink and Yellow Rose Spray (Rose Cluster), GST3 and gold trim
1948	Italian Rose, blue trim
1950	Same as Scroll Border, but with a larger center decal
1952	Pink Begonia, gold band edge, gold verge line
1954	Pink Begonia, GST42 and gold trim
1956	Buttercup, gold trim
1958	Cabbage Rose, GST52 and gold trim
1960	Pink Begonia, GST52 and gold trim
1961	Cabbage Rose, PST52 and platinum trim
1966	ST: GST53 with gold trim
1968	Glamour, gold trim
1969	Forget-me-not, gold edge
1972	Pink Begonia, gold trim, GST53 and gold trim

Treatment	Name and/or Description
1974	Mayfair, two-tone, gold trim and brown encasing line
1976	Cabbage Rose, GST25 and gold trim
1977	ST: GST4 with gold trim
1978	ST: GST7 with gold trim
1979	ST: GST59 with gold trim
1980	ST: GST39 with gold trim
1981	Cabbage Rose, GST39 and gold trim
1987	Buttercup, yellow edge line, brown drop line
1989	Blue Leaf Rose, blue and salmon bands
1990	Pine Cone, green and brown bands
1992	Pink and Yellow Rose Spray (Rose Cluster), green and pink bands
1993	Pink Begonia, pink and gray bands
1997	BT: red edge band, red line on teapots only
1998	BT: green edge band, green line on teapots only
1999	BT: blue edge band, blue line on teapots only
2000	BT: heavy red band on teapots only
2001	Scrap prints used on chop plates (Lu-Ray shape)
2002	Scrap prints used on salad bowls (Lu-Ray shape)
2003	Pink and Yellow Rose Spray (Rose Cluster), GST53 and gold trim
2004	Blue Leaf Rose, GST53 and gold trim
2007	Blue Leaf Rose, GST39 and gold trim
2008	Pink and Yellow Rose Spray (Rose Cluster), GST39 and gold trim
2030	Italian Rose, gray band, pink line
2031	Italian Rose, green band, pink line
2032	Buttercup, gray band, green line
2033	Buttercup, blue band, green line
2052	Diana, Dresden Rose with GST23
2053	LRT: Chatham Modern, Chartreuse
2054	LRT: Chatham Modern, Gray
2055	LRT: Chatham Modern, Brown
2056	LRT: Chatham Modern, Jade
2057	Pink Begonia, gold trim
2059	Apple Blossom, green line on flange OR two-tone green, no trim
2060	LRT: Coffee Tree, Lu-Ray gray, NEL
2061	LRT: Sea Shells, Lu-Ray gray, NEL
2064	LRT: Chatham Modern, Red
2065	LRT: Marsh Violet, Lu-Ray gray, NEL
2066	Rosemont, no trim
2068	LRT: Chatham Modern, Gray
2069	Blue Leaf Rose with stamp border
2071	Blue Leaf Rose with pink line on flange

Treatment	Name and/or Description
2072	Pink and Yellow Rose Spray (Rose Cluster), blue line on flange
2073	LRT: Chatham Modern, Yellow
2074	LRT: Chatham Modern, Green
2075	LRT: Chatham Modern, Maroon
2076	LRT: Chatham Modern, Brown
2077	LRT: Chatham Modern, Red
2078	LRT: Chatham Modern, Green
2079	LRT: Chatham Modern, Platinum
2080	LRT: Chatham Modern, Gray
2081	LRT: Chatham Modern, Turquoise
2082	LRT: Chatham Modern, Light Red
2083	LRT: Chatham Modern, Golden Brown
2084	LRT: Chatham Modern, Mauve
2085	LRT: Jack in Pulpit on Lu-Ray gray, NEL
2086	Blue Leaf Rose, gold lace stamp and gold trim
2087	Pink and Yellow Rose Spray (Rose Cluster), gold lace stamp and gold trim
2090	ST: "Masterpiece" PST60 with platinum edge and body lines
2091	Marsh Violet, GST57
2092	Blue Leaf Rose, GST53 and gold trim
2094	Cabbage Rose, GST55, GST9, and GST26 with gold band
2095	Cabbage Rose, GST32 with gold trim
2096	Lady Godey, Godey
2101	Cabbage Rose, ST23
2105	Cabbage Rose, ST13
2106	Cabbage Rose, ST57
2112	Marsh Violet, GST55, GST9 and GST26
2113	Rosemont, gold band and gold stamp
2114	Gold Greek Key
2123	Carnation, 3s, gold trim
2126	Buttercup, 1s, gold trim
2127	Coffee Tree, brown EL
2128	Sea Shells, pink EL
2129	Marsh Violet, green EL
2130	Rosemont, green edge line
2131	Colonial Kitchen, gold trim
2132	Woolworth Rose, gold trim
2133	Rosemont, dark green two-tone
2135	Woolworth Rose, dark green two-tone
2136	Woolworth Rose, gray drop band
2137	ST: GST57 with gold trim
2139	Blue Leaf Rose with GST42
2142	Buttercup, 3s, gold trim
2143	Woolworth Rose, gold trim
2144	Daylily, green edge line
2145	Magnolia, gray edge line

Treatment	Name and/or Description	Treatment	Name and/or Description
2146	Woolworth Rose, Beauty Rose, Rhythm Rose, green edge line	2203	Dogwood, two-tone green, gold trim
2147	Italian Rose, maroon edge line	2204	Swan Flower, Laurel two-tone green, gold trim ("Bonnie")
2149	Coffee Tree, Con two-tone green, gold trim and encasing line	2205	Lady Camille (Dogwood), GST23
2150	Marsh Violet, Con two-tone green, gold trim and encasing line	2206	ST: GST34 on verge with gold edge band and gold verge
2151	ST: GST23 on dark green two-tone body, no decal and no trim	2207	Begonia, Laurel two-tone green with gold trim.
2152	Colonial Kitchen, GST23, no trim	2208	Italian Rose, gold trim
2153	ST: large portion of ST58 in platinum with platinum edge and body lines	2209	Marsh Violet, green edge and verge lines
2159	Blue Leaf Rose, GST52 and gold trim	2210	Begonia, gold trim and green band
2160	ST: GST47	2211	Bahama, brown edge and verge
2161	Coffee Tree, gold trim	2212	Nassau (Trinidad), brown edge and verge
2162	Dresden Rose, two-tone green	2214	Herb Garden, lace stamp
2163	Lady Godey, ST27	2118	Marsh Violet, two-tone green, GST27
2164	Woolworth Rose, ST23	2219	Woolworth Rose, two-tone green, SGT27
2165	Marsh Violet, ST27	2220	Dresden center, two-tone green, GST27
2166	Petunia, ST27 and gold trim	2221	Swiss Provincial, no trim
2167	Colonial Kitchen, green edge line	2222	Sea Shells, 1s, gold trim
2168	Marsh Violet, green edge line	2223	Colonial Kitchen, GST27, no trim
2169	Woolworth Rose, blue-green band	2224	Shalimar Rose (Woolworth Rose) GST23
2170	Petunia, green band	2225	Marsh Violet, gold trim
2172	Woolworth Rose, GST3	2226	Rosemont
2176	Lady Godey, (sold as "Richelieu"), GST44 and GST23	2227	Swiss Provincial, two-tone yellow
2177	Marsh Violet, GST39	2229	Dogwood, platinum trim
2178	Colonial Kitchen, GST27	2230	Dogwood, gold trim
2179	Lady Helene, GST27	2231	Woolworth Rose
2180	Marsh Violet, green edge line	2233	Woolworth Rose
2181	Buttercup, 1s, gold trim	2235	ST: rose stamp on two-tone blue
2182	Carnation, GST27	2236	ST: chicken track stamp on two-tone blue
2183	Colonial Kitchen, gold trim	2237	Pennsylvania Dutch, no trim
2184	Lady Helene, green edge line	2238	Jamaica, gold trim
2185	Rosemont, green edge line	2239	Lady Helene, platinum trim
2186	Nassau, dark brown edge	2240	Begonia, gold trim
2187	Woolworth Rose, Platinum band	2241	Woolworth Rose, gold trim
2192	Woolworth Rose, platinum trim	2242	Winter Scene, gold stamp
2193	Apple Blossom (sold as "Golden Lace"), GST23	2243	Winter Scene, gold stamp
2194	Begonia, lace stamp	2246	Bleu Claire, two-tone blue, gold trim
2195	Colonial Kitchen, gold lace stamp, no trim	2247	Indian Summer on Versatile two-tone Coral, gold trim
2196	Dogwood, two-tone green, lace stamp	2248	Indian Summer on Versatile two-tone Coral, gold trim and encasing line
2197	Dogwood, two-tone green, GST23	2249	Swan Flower, Versatile two-tone Green, gold trim and encasing line.
2198	Conversation white with lace stamp, no decal	2250	Begonia, gold stamp
2199	Lady Godey, Conversation two-tone green with lace stamp	2251	Dogwood, platinum trim
		2252	Dogwood, platinum trim
2202	Tropicana, Jamaica, no trim	2253	Herb Garden, platinum trim
		2255	Italian Rose, platinum trim

2256	ST: platinum stamp with platinum trim
2257	Winter Scene, two-tone blue, lace stamp
2258	Winter Scene, two-tone green, lace stamp
2259	Winter Scene, two-tone coral, lace stamp
2260	Begonia, platinum trim
2261	Woolworth Rose, two-tone green
2262	ST: lace stamp
2263	Jamaica, no trim
2265	Berry Cluster, gold edge line
2267	Nosegay, gold edge line
2268	Blue Claire, gold edge line
2273	Apple Blossom, platinum trim
2278	Lady Helene, platinum trim
2279	Nosegay, two-tone green, gold trim
2280	Rosemont, two-tone green, laces stamp
2281	Yellow Wheat, two-tone yellow, gold trim
2282	Carnation, 3s, gold trim
2285	Buttercup, 3s, no trim
2286	Apple Blossom, gold trim
2289	Acacia, 3s, two-tone yellow
2291	Swan Flower, platinum trim
2292	Marsh Violet, platinum trim
2299	Berry Cluster
2300	Dogwood
2304	Mardi Gras
2305	Swan Flower (with stamp border)
2307	Morning Glory
2308	Blue Mist
2309	Silver Mist
2310	Dresden
2324	Dwarf Pine (Ming)
2325	Silver Sprig
2328	Moulin Rouge
2330	Blue Twig
2335	Harvest Gold
2336	Summer Night (Dwarf Pine on blue Versatile)
2340	Dawn
2341	Bittersweet, platinum trim
2349	Stem Rose, Fern Rose, gold trim
2352	Delightful
2353	Dwarf Pine
2357	Pin Oak
2359	Mardi Gras on white Versatile
2360	Leaf O' Gold
2361	Bittersweet
2362	Dawn
2366	Leaf O' Gold
2367	Dwarf Pine
2371	White Wheat

2373	Shasta Daisy
2374	Meadow Mist
2383	Bachelor Button
2384	Carnation
2385	Blue Lace
2386	Pepperwood
2387	Monticello
2397	Leaf of Gold
2399	Majestic
2401	Silver Spruce
2404	Gold-n-Spray
2407	Pink Sachet, Forrest Pink
2408	Blue Meadow
2422	Petal Lane, Jubilee
2430	Dianthus
2434	Petal Lane, Jubilee
2442	Blue Twig

Appendix II: Values

Early TST Dinnerware Lines
Navarre, Normandie, Savoy, Latona, Verona, Avona, Pennova, and Belva

Teacup	$4-5
Tea saucer	$1-2
Coffee cup	$4-5
Coffee saucer	$1-2
Demitasse cup	$5-6
Demitasse saucer	$2-3
Bouillon cup	$5-6
Bouillon saucer	$2-3
36s bowl	$5-6
30s bowl	$5-6
Jugs, any size	$8-10
Teapot, 8-cup	$20-25
Teapot, 6-cup	$20-25
Regular sugar	$5-7
Demitasse sugar	$8-9
Regular creamer	$4-5
Demitasse creamer	$6-8
Large covered casserole	$15-20
Medium covered casserole	$12-18
Sauceboat	$6-8
Sauceboat stand	$4-5
Gravy fast-stand	$6-8
Covered butter, round	$10-12
10" oval baker	$6-8
9" oval baker	$5-7
8" oval baker	$5-7

7" oval baker	$6-8
10" nappy	$6-8
9" nappy	$5-7
8" nappy	$5-7
7" nappy	$6-8
Lug round platters, any size	$8-10
17" platter	$12-15
15" platter	$10-12
13" platter	$10-12
11" platter	$7-9
9" platter	$5-8
7" platter	$5-8
10" plate	$7-9
9" plate	$5-6
8" plate	$7-9
7" plate	$3-4
6" plate	$1-2
5" fruit cup	$2-3
6" oatmeal	$2-3
8" rim soup	$4-6
Bone dish	$8-10
Covered sauce dish	$15-18
Spoon boat	$8-10
Butter pat	$7-9

TST Early Art Ware and Specialties

Spittoon, Fargo	$20-25
Spittoon, Okla	$20-25
8 1/2" Calcutta bowl	$8-10
9-3/4" Sydney bowl	$8-10
Shell Salad bowl	$18-20
Florodora Orange bowl	$20-25
Brussels Salad bowl	$8-10
Brussels large plate	$8-10
Brussels small plate	$5-8
Paris plaque	$8-10
London plaque	$12-15
Normandie plaque	$8-10
Lace plate	$5-8
Rome nut bowl	$7-9
Cairo bowl	$8-10
Chocolate pot	$30-35
Cracker jar	$30-35
Celery tray	$10-12
Olive dish	$10-12
Jumbo coffee cup	$8-10
Jumbo coffee saucer	$2-3
Sitka bowl, 9"	$8-10
Sitka bowl, 6"	$4-6
Beer mug, Bohemian, Jr.	$10-12

Beer mug, Bohemian, Sr.	$15-18
Tankard (tall pitcher)	$35-40

Hotel, Cable, & Utility Ware

Hospital tray	$10-12
Compartment plate	$8-10
Ice tub, two hoops	$18-20
Hall Boy Jugs, any size	$8-10
Rocaille Jugs, any size	$15-18
Dutch Jugs, any size	$12-15
Handled mug, ale	$8-10
Handled mug, hot soda	$8-10
Boston egg cup	$8-10
Poached egg cup	$6-8
Tumbler, 7 oz.	$8-10
Tumbler, 8 oz.	$10-12
Gem teacup	$4-5
Gen saucer	$1-2
Hotel sugar	$10-12
Hotel mustard	$10-12
Chester teacup	$4-5
Chester saucer	$1-2
Cable egg cup	$7-9
Cable mug	$3-5
Cable jugs, any size	$8-10
Cable sugar	$8-10
Cable sauceboat	$4-6
Cable covered butter	$8-10
Cable butter pat	$4-6
Cable platters, any size	$5-7
Cable plates, any size	$4-6
Cable bakers and nappies	$7-9
Cable fruits and oatmeals	$4-5
Spittoon, Chester shape	$10-15

Toilet Ware
Pittsburg, Chicago, New York, Hotel, & Plain

Ewer	$15-20
Basin	$15-20
Pitcher	$12-15
Chamber pot	$20-25
Combinet	$30-35
Brush jar	$8-10
Mug	$8-10
Soap dish, with drainer	$12-15
Slop jar	$20-25
Juvenile Ewer	$25-30
Juvenile Basin	$25-30
Juvenile chamber pot	$35-40

Soap dish, slab	$8-10		Salt box	$18-20
Hospital urinal	$8-10		Creamer	$5-8

Soap dish, slab $8-10
Hospital urinal $8-10

Salt box $18-20
Creamer $5-8
Barbeque plate $8-10
6-3/4" ashtray $12-15
6" ashtray $12-15
Range shakers, pair $18-20
Teapot $20-25
Bean pot $25-30
Sugar, wooden lid $8-10
Flite Haven bird houses, any style   UND

Capitol

10" plate $6-8
9" plate $5-7
8" plate $6-8
7" plate $5-7
6" plate $4-6
Teacup $4-6
Saucer $1-2
15" platter $8-10
13" platter $6-8
11" platter $5-7
9" platter $5-7
Nappy, any size $6-8
Baker, any size $5-7
Covered casserole $12-15
Teapot $15-20
Sugar $6-8
Creamer $4-6
Sauceboat $5-7
Gravy fast-stand $8-10
24s jug $10-12
Lug soup $5-8
Rim soup $7-9
Fruit cup $2-3
Oatmeal bowl $4-6
36s bowl $5-8
Covered butter $10-12
Special Nestlé's® cup & saucer $10-12

Design 70

10" Plate $4-6
8" Plate $3-5
6" Plate $1-2
Cup $2-3
Saucer $1-2
Coupe soup $3-5
Fruit $2-3
Covered sugar $5-6
Creamer $4-5
Rice bowl $2-3
Covered butter $6-8
Divided relish $8-10
13" oval platter $7-9
Coffeepot $10-12
Large vegetable $5-7
Medium vegetable $4-6
Divided vegetable $6-8
Serving casserole $7-9
Cooking casserole $10-12
Pickle $4-6
17" bread tray $12-15
Teapot $15-18
Milk pitcher $10-12
Shakers, pair $8-10
Oil & Vinegar $15-18
15" salad bowl $8-10
Ladle $6-8
Ramekin $5-7
Sauceboat and tray $6-8

Chateau Buffet

Le Saladier $15-20
Fork $8-10
Spoon $8-10
Les Assiettes A Salade $15-20
La Grande Terrine $15-20
La Terrine Moyenne $12-15
Les Ramequins $5-8
La Carafe $10-12
Cup $4-6
Saucer $2-3
Dinner plate $7-9
Coffee server (wooden handle) $15-18
Covered casserole $15-20
Hot chocolate mug (Taylor mug) $7-9
Cereal bowl $4-6
Ramekin $4-6
Covered butter $12-15

Classic

10" plate $5-7
8" plate $4-6
6" plate $3-4
Teacup $4-6
Saucer $1-2
Covered sugar $6-8
Creamer $3-4

Sauceboat	$6-8		Gravy fast-stand	$8-10
Gravy fast-stand	$6-8		Fruit cup	$2-3
Coffeepot	$15-18		Oatmeal bowl	$4-5
Pepper shaker	$4-5		Lug soup	$5-7
Salt shaker	$4-5		Rim soup	$5-7
Chop plate	$6-8		Covered casserole	$15-20
Oval platter	$6-8		Covered vegetable (Beverly)	$10-12
Lug soup	$5-7		Teapot	$18-20
Baker	$4-6		Covered butter	$20-25
Nappy	$4-6		Creamer	$4-5
Covered casserole, with foot	$18-20		Sugar	$6-8
Covered casserole, without foot	$18-20		Teacup	$2-3
Covered tureen	$20-25		Saucer	$1-2
			Nappy	$6-8
			Baker	$5-7

Conversation

Empire & Laurel

13" chop plate	$8-10		10" plate	$8-10
10" plate	$6-8		9" plate	$6-8
8" plate	$6-8		8" plate	$8-10
6" plate	$3-4		7" plate	$5-7
Fruit cup	$3-4		6" plate	$4-5
Oatmeal bowl	$5-6		Chop plate	$10-12
Rim soup	$6-8		9" round nappy	$6-8
Covered sugar	$8-10		9" oval baker	$6-8
Creamer	$5-7		10" oval baker	$8-10
Teacup	$4-6		15" platter	$10-12
Tea saucer	$1-2		13" platter	$8-10
Demitasse cup	$8-10		11" platter	$5-7
Demitasse saucer	$2-3		7" platter	$8-10
Shakers, pair	$6-8		Pickle, sauceboat stand	$7-9
Oval baker	$7-9		Fruit cup	$3-4
Nappy	$7-9		Oatmeal bowl	$4-5
Covered casserole	$10-12		Rim soup	$5-7
Service jug	$15-18		Lug soup	$5-7
Coffeepot	$15-18		36s bowl	$12-15
13" platter	$8-10		Creamer	$4-5
11" platter	$6-8		Covered sugar	$6-8
Sauceboat	$8-10		Demitasse creamer, Empire	$12-15
Sauceboat stand	$7-9		Demitasse sugar, Empire	$18-20
			Teacup, Laurel	$4-5
Delphian & Beverly			Teacup, Empire	$12-15
			Tea saucer	$1-2
			Demitasse cup	$8-10
10" plate	$6-8		Demitasse saucer	$4-5
9" plate	$5-7		Demitasse coffeepot, Empire	$40-50
8" plate	$6-8		Covered butter, round, Laurel	$35-40
7" plate	$4-6		Covered butter, stick, Empire	$18-20
6" plate	$3-4		Covered casserole	$20-25
15" platter	$8-10		Jug, with foot	$20-25
13" platter	$6-8		Jug, without foot	$15-20
11" platter	$6-8			
9" platter	$5-7			
Gravy	$5-7			

Gravy fast-stand	$10-12
Teapot, Laurel	$15-18
Teapot, flat spout, Empire	$20-25
Teapot, curved spout, Empire	$15-20
Eggcup	$7-9
Muffin cover	$15-20
Compartment plate	$8-10
Cream soup cup	$8-10
Cream soup liner	$5-7
Shakers, pr.	$8-10
Lug cake plate	$7-9

Ever Yours

Cup	$2-3
Saucer	$1-2
6" plate	$1-2
7" plate	$2-3
8" plate	$4-5
10" plate	$5-6
Fruit	$1-2
Coupe soup	$4-5
Lug soup	$4-5
11 1/2" platter	$6-8
13" platter	$8-10
Large vegetable	$7-9
Medium vegetable	$7-9
Covered sugar	$6-8
Creamer	$4-5
Coffeepot	$12-15
Covered butter	$8-10
Salt and pepper	$8-10
14" chop plate	$10-12
Water jug	$18-20
Sauceboat	$8-10
Casserole	$12-15
Divided vegetable	$7-9
Pickle	$6-8
Teapot	$18-20
Chip & Dip bowl	$6-8
Chip & Dip plate	$8-10
Cake plate (Laurel)	$7-9
Cake lifter	$10-12
Carafe	$12-15

Fairway

10" plate	$6-8
9" plate	$5-7
7" plate	$4-6
6" plate	$3-4
Teacup	$4-6

Tea saucer	$1-2
Creamer	$3-4
Sugar, open	$7-9
Sugar, covered	$7-9
Covered casserole	$12-15
Sauceboat	$8-10
13" platter	$8-10
11" platter	$6-8
5" fruit cup	$1-2
6" oatmeal	$2-3
Rim soup	$4-6
Lug soup	$4-6
Nappy	$5-7
9" oval baker	$5-7
10" oval baker	$6-8

Garland

10" plate	$6-8
9" plate	$5-7
7" plate	$4-6
6" plate	$3-4
Teacup	$3-4
Tea saucer	$1-2
Teapot	$20-25
Covered casserole	$18-20
Covered sugar	$8-10
Creamer	$5-6
Baker	$6-8
Nappy	$6-8
Covered nappy	$10-12
13" platter	$8-10
11" platter	$6-8
Sauceboat	$8-10
Pickle, sauceboat stand	$4-6
Lug cake plate	$7-9
5" fruit cup	$1-2
6" oatmeal	$3-4
Rim soup	$6-8

Granada

Cup	$2-3
Saucer	$1-2
6" plate	$1-2
8" plate	$3-4
10" plate	$5-6
Dessert bowl	$1-2
Cereal bowl	$2-3
Vegetable bowl	$4-6
13" platter	$6-8
11" platter, round	$5-7

11" platter, oval	$5-7
Creamer	$4-6
Sugar	$6-8
Sauceboat	$6-8
Sauceboat stand	$4-6
Coffee pot	$10-12
Casserole	$8-10
Covered butter	$8-10
Shakers, pair	$7-9
Teapot	$15-20
Oil	$7-9
Vinegar	$7-9
Oval baker	$4-6
Milk jug	$7-9
Divided vegetable	$5-8

Holly & Spruce

10" plate	$6-8
Cup	$4-6
Saucer	$2-3
Cake plate	$4-6
Salad plate	$5-7
Cup O' Cheer	$4-6
Punch bowl	$12-15
Punch bowl with wooden stand & plastic ladle	$18-20
Holly ashtray, large	$10-12
Holly ashtray, small	$8-10
Triangular ashtray	$12-15
Nutmeg shaker	$8-10
Welled plate, round	$7-9
Welled plate, shell	$12-15
Divided relish tray	$12-15
Milk jug	$15-18
Deviled-Egg plate	$20-25
Two-tiered tidbit, wooden handles	$12-15
Two-tiered tidbit, metal handles	$12-15
Irish Coffee	UND
Cookie jar	$45-50
Coffee server	$30-35
Creamer	$7-9
Sugar	$10-12
Bon-bon dish	$15-18
Covered casserole	$30-35

Juvenile China

Item	Kate Greenway, Tiny Todkins & Brownies, any shape	Other Treatments
6" plate	$10-12	$8-10
Teacup	$8-10	$6-8
Saucer	$4-5	$1-2
Fruit cup	$6-8	$5-7
Oatmeal bowl	$8-10	$5-7
Teapot	$85-95	$55-75
Casserole	$85-95	$60-80
Sugar	$20-25	$15-18
Creamer	$18-20	$10-12
Spoon boat	$20-25	$15-18
Butter pat	$12-15	$10-12
36s bowl	$20-25	$10-15
Mug	$15-20	$10-12
Tumbler	$25-30	$12-15
Platter	$20-25	$15-18
Baby Bunting dishes, any treatment		$20-25
Holdfast baby dish, by TST		$25-30
Holdfast baby dish, by McNicol		$30-35

Breakfast Sets

Item	Popeye & Howdy Doody	Other Treatments
Plate	$20-25	$10-12
Mug	$15-20	$8-10
Bowl	$20-25	$10-12

Lu-Ray Pastels

Item	Approx. Dates of Production	4 Original Colors	Chatham Gray
10" plate	1938-1961	$20-25	$30-35
9" plate	1938-1961	$12-15	$20-25
8" plate	1938-1961	$20-25	$45-50
7" plate	1938-1961	$9-12	$20-25
6" plate	1938-1961	$7-9	$15-20

Item	Approx. Dates of Production	4 Original Colors	Chatham Gray
Chop plate	1938-1955	$40-50	$275+
Compartment plate	1941-1955	$30-35	$100-125
Teacup	1938-1961	$8-10	$25-30
Tea saucer	1938-1961	$3-4	$8-10
Demitasse cup	1940-1955	$25-30	$40-45
Demitasse saucer	1940-1955	$12-15	$15-18
Chocolate cup	1939-1940	$100+	NA
Chocolate saucer	1939-1940	$50-55	NA
Creamer, regular	1938-1961	$10-12	$40-45
Creamer, demitasse	1939-1940	$45-50	NA
Creamer, chocolate	1940-1945	$300+	NA
Sugar, regular	1938-1955	$22-25	$75-85
Sugar, demitasse	1940-1945	$65-75	NA
Sugar, chocolate	1939-1940	$400+	NA
Sugar, no handles	1955-1961	$45-50	NA
Teapot, flat spout	1938-1941	$125-145	NA
Teapot, curved spout	1941-1955	$85-95	$250+
Covered casserole	1938-1945	$90-110	NA
Nappy	1938-1961	$18-20	$45-50
Baker	1938-1961	$18-20	$45-55
Fruit cup	1938-1961	$6-8	$30-35
36s bowl	1938-1955	$55-60	$125+
Rim soup	1938-1961	$15-18	$40-45
13" platter	1938-1961	$20-22	$40-45
11" platter	1938-1961	$20-22	$40-45
Pickle/sauceboat stand	1938-1945	$35-40	NA
Double eggcup	1939-1955	$25-30	$80-85
Lug soup	1938-1955	$18-20	$50-55
Cream soup cup	1938-1945	$45-50	NA
Cream soup liner	1938-1945	$18-20	NA
Covered butter dish	1941-1955	$65-70	$160+
Salad bowl	1941-1945	$65-70	$250+
Jug, footed	1938-1941	$100-125	NA
Jug, no foot	1941-1955	$85-100	*
Juice pitcher	1941-1945	$125-135	NA
Juice tumbler	1941-1945	$70-80	NA
Water tumbler	1942-1945	$70-80	NA
Muffin cover	1940-1945	$90-100	NA
Gravy fast-stand	1938-1955	$40-45	*
Sauceboat	1938-1945	$25-30	NA
Demitasse pot	1940-1945	$185-200	NA
Chocolate pot	1939-1940	$650+	NA
Handled cake plate	1938-1945	$65-75	NA
Shakers, pair	1938-1961	$20-25	$40-45
4-part relish	1938-1942	$95-100	NA
10" mixing bowl	1941-1942	$200+	NA
8" mixing bowl	1941-1942	$200+	NA
7" mixing bowl	1941-1942	$200+	NA
5" mixing bowl	1941-1942	$200+	NA
Flower vase (epergne)	1939-1942	$250+	NA
Bud urn	1939-1942	$250+	NA
Bud vase	1939-1942	$250+	NA
Nut dish/coaster	1942-1945	$95-110	NA

Marvel

Item	Approx. Dates of Production	4 Original Colors	Chatham Gray
10" plate			$6-8
9" plate			$5-7
8" plate			$6-8
7" plate			$5-7
6" plate			$4-5

Teacup	$4-5
Saucer	$2-3
Oval baker	$4-6
Round nappy	$4-6
9" platter	$5-7
11" platter	$6-8
13" platter	$8-10
15" platter	$10-12
Double egg cup	$12-15
Casserole, original	$10-12
Casserole, restyled	$18-20
Sugar, original	$5-7
Sugar, restyled	$8-10
Creamer, original	$4-6
Creamer, restyled	$6-8
Teapot, original	$30-35
Teapot, restyled	$40-45
Sauceboat, original	$6-8
Sauceboat, restyled	$10-12
Covered butter, original	$10-12
Covered butter, restyled	$18-20

Octagon

10" plate	$4-5
8" plate	$3-4
6" plate	$1-2
Teacup	$3-4
Saucer	$1-2
Sugar	$6-8
Creamer	$3-4
Vegetable bowl	$5-7
Shakers, pair	$6-8

Paramount & Regal

10" plate	$7-9
9" plate	$6-8
8" plate	$7-9
7" plate	$5-6
6" plate	$4-5
Fruit cup	$3-4
Oatmeal bowl	$4-5
36s bowl	$10-12
Rim soup	$6-8
Cream soup cup	$6-8
Cream soup liner	$3-4
Compartment plate	$10-12
Handled tray, with well	$12-15
Handled tray, without well	$10-12
17" platter	$12-15

15" platter	$10-12
13" platter	$8-10
11" platter	$8-10
9" platter	$6-8
Pickle	$5-6
Cover for the 11" platter	$12-15
Batter jug	$20-25
Syrup pitcher	$18-20
Sauceboat	$8-10
Gravy fast-stand	$10-12
Creamer	$4-6
Sugar	$5-8
Teacup, tall	$4-6
Teacup, short	$4-6
Saucer	$1-2
Covered casserole	$20-25
Teapot	$30-35
Muffin cover	$20-25
Butter dish	$12-15
10" nappy	$6-8
9" nappy	$5-7
10" baker	$6-8
9" baker	$5-7

Pebbleford

12" chop plate	$15-18
10" plate	$10-12
7" plate	$6-8
6" plate	$4-6
11" platter	$10-12
13" platter	$12-15
Teacup, regular	$5-8
Teacup, Empire	$15-18
Teacup, Castilian	$10-12
Saucer	$2-3
Sugar with handles	$12-15
Sugar without handles	$10-12
Sugar, Empire	$18-20
Sugar, Ever Yours	$15-18
Creamer, regular	$6-8
Creamer, Empire	$12-15
Creamer, Castilian	$10-12
Creamer, Ever Yours	$10-12
Sauceboat	$12-15
Shakers, regular	$10-12
Shakers, Castilian	$12-15
Covered casserole	$18-20
Divided baker	$15-18
Oval vegetable	$10-12
Round serving bowl	$10-12

Coupe soup	$8-10
Pickle	$9-12
Fruit cup	$4-6
10" mixing bowl	$100+
8" mixing bowl	$100+
7" mixing bowl	$100+
5" mixing bowl	$100+
Lug soup	$8-10
Lug soup lid	$15-18
Egg cup	$15-20
Covered butter with finial	$18-20
Covered butter without finial	$20-25
Covered cheese dish	$55-65
Water jug	$35-40
Teapot	$40-45
Coffee pot, 3" opening	$30-35
Coffee pot, 4" opening	$30-35
Coffee pot, Classic	$40-45
Covered cigarette box	$85+
Cake lifter	$20-25
Coffee carafe, Ever Yours	$25-30
Relish, Ever Yours	$15-18
Shell snack plate	$20-25
Taylor barbeque mug	$10-15
Chateau buffet bowl	$10-15
Small French casserole	$10-15
Therma-Role	$300+
Cookie jar	$250+
Canister, first size	UND
Canister, second size	UND
Canister, third size	UND
Canister, fourth size	UND

Plymouth

Teapot, 6-cup	$25-30
Teapot, 8-cup	$25-30
10" plate	$7-9
9" plate	$6-8
8" plate	$7-9
7" plate	$5-7
6" plate	$3-4
Lug soup	$4-6
Covered vegetable	$10-12
Covered casserole	$20-25
Console bowl	$25-30
Candleholders, pr.	$20-25
Shakers, pr.	$10-12
Sauceboat	$8-10
Sugar	$8-10
Creamer	$6-8
Pickle	$6-8

Fast-stand	$10-12
Cream soup cup	$10-12
Cream soup liner	$4-6
Covered butter, round	$18-20
Teacup	$4-6
Tea saucer	$1-2
Demitasse cup	$6-8
Demitasse saucer	$2-3
36s bowl	$8-10
Soup bowl	$5-7
Oatmeal bowl	$4-6
Fruit cup	$3-4
Coaster	$10-12
8" nappy	$6-8
9" nappy	$6-8
10" nappy	$7-9
Baker	$10-12
11" lug chop plate	$10-12
13" lug chop plate	$12-15
15" lug chop plate	$15-18

Quaker Oats

Harvest, Wild Rose, Pastoral, Fortune, and Modern Star patterns:

6" plate	$2-3
Teacup	$2-3
Saucer	$1-2
Fruit cup	$1-2
Oatmeal bowl	$2-3

Oven Serve, Chateau Buffet, & Rooster:

Cereal bowl	$2-3
French casserole	$3-4
Custard	$1-2
Ramekin	$2-4
Baker (Oven Serve only)	$4-6

Scalloped Rim

10" plate	$6-8
9" plate	$5-7
7" plate	$4-6
6" plate	$1-2
Teacup	$4-6
Tea saucer	$1-2
Teapot	$30-35
Covered casserole	$20-25
Covered sugar	$7-9
Creamer	$4-6
13" platter	$10-12

11" platter	$7-9	Coupe soup	$18-20
Sauceboat	$8-10	Lug soup	$20-25
Pickle, sauceboat stand	$5-7	5" fruit cup	$8-10
Lug cake plate	$10-12	8 1/2" nappy	$40-45
Nappy	$7-9	12" chop platter	$35-40
Baker	$7-9	15" chop platter	$55-60
5" fruit cup	$1-2	Creamer	$15-20
6" oatmeal	$2-3	Sugar	$25-30
Rim soup	$5-7	Teapot	$125+
Covered butter	$15-18	Footed salad, ruffled foot	$250+
		Footed salad, plain foot	$200-225

Versatile

		Water jug	$85-110
		Sauceboat	$250+
Teacup	$2-3	Shakers, pr.	$15-20
Saucer	$1-2	Egg cup	$45-50
10" plate	$6-8	AD coffee cup	$30-35
8" plate	$5-7	AD coffee saucer	$12-15
6" plate	$1-2		
Coupe soup	$4-6	**Vogue**	
Lug soup	$6-8		
Fruit cup	$1-2	10" plate	$8-10
11" platter	$7-9	9" plate	$6-8
13" platter	$8-10	8" plate, round	$8-10
Medium nappy	$8-10	8" plate, square	$8-10
Large nappy	$7-9	7" plate	$4-6
Baker	$7-9	6" plate	$2-3
Sugar	$7-9	Teacup	$4-6
Creamer	$3-4	Saucer	$1-2
Tall creamer	$10-12	15" platter	$15-18
Handled soups		13" platter	$10-12
(French casseroles)	$10-12	11" platter	$10-12
Cake plate (Laurel shape)	$8-10	9" platter	$7-9
Teapot	$20-25	Sauceboat	$8-10
Coffeepot	$18-20	Gravy fast-stand	$10-12
Shakers, pr.	$6-8	Covered casserole	$20-25
Sauceboat	$7-9	Sugar	$8-10
Casserole	$12-15	Creamer, wide opening	$8-10
Pickle	$7-9	Creamer, regular opening	$6-8
Covered butter	$10-12	Lug soup	$6-8
Divided baker	$7-9	Fruit cup	$2-3
Chop plate	$8-10	Oatmeal bowl	$4-6
		36s bowl	$10-12
Vistosa		Soup	$7-9
		Baker, any size	$7-9
Teacup	$12-15	Nappy, any size	$7-9
Tea saucer	$3-4	Lug cake plate, with rim	$7-9
10" plate	$45-50	Lug cake plate, without rim	$10-12
9" plate	$15-20	Covered butter	$20-25
7" plate	$10-12	Teapot	$30-35
6" plate	$8-10		

Other TST Shapes & Patterns: Taylorton

Round platter	$10-12
Oval platter	$8-10
10" plate	$6-8
9" plate	$5-7
7" plate	$4-6
6" plate	$3-4
Large vegetable	$5-7
Medium vegetable	$4-6
Bread tray	$12-15
Relish tray	$8-10
Salt server/ashtray	$4-6
Casserole	$15-20
Coffee pot	$15-20
Salt shaker	$4-6
Pepper shaker	$4-6
Cup	$2-3
Saucer	$1-2
Desert bowl	$1-2
Soup/cereal	$2-.3
Soup cup	$4-5
Sugar	$6-8
Creamer	$5-7
Sauceboat	$8-10
Sauceboat tray	$4-6
Oil	$10-12
Vinegar	$10-12
Buffet salt	$8-10
Pepper mill	$8-10

For Ranchero, Taylorstone, Sierra, Heathertone, Colorcraft, Aunt Jenny's, Shades of Grandeur, & Dogwood, use the following:

Large pieces such as platters, dinner plates, & serving bowls:	$7-9
Small pieces such as cups, saucers, 6" plates, small bowls:	$4-6
Large hollowware (coffeepots, teapots, casseroles, etc.):	$12-15
Small hollowware (sugars, creamers, shakers, etc.):	$5-8

Miscellaneous

Soup tureen	$20-25
Cigarette box	$25-30
Apple cookie jar	$20-25
Apple grease jar	$25-30
Apple salt shaker	$10-15
Apple pepper shaker	$10-15

Howdy Doody cookie jar	$250+
State plates	$7-10
Leaf Fantasy plate	$15-20
Leaf Fantasy cup	$10-12
George and Martha, plates less than 10"	$10-12
George and Martha, plates 10" or more	$18-20
Souvenir Ashtrays	$5-8
Naughty Ashtrays	$8-10
Promotional coasters	$6-8
Advertising pins	$12-15
Salad bowls	$10-12
Shell snack plates, Pebbleford glazes	$20-25
Shell snack plates, Holly & Spruce	$12-15
Shell snack plates, any other decoration	$8-10
1930s chocolate pot	$40-50
1930s chocolate creamer	$15-20
1930s chocolate sugar	$20-25
1930s chocolate cup	$8-10
1930s chocolate saucer	$4-6

(For prices of the chocolate sets in Lu-Ray glazes, see section on Lu-Ray Pastels.)

(For prices of the Empire demitasse set, see section on Empire & Laurel.)

Bicentennial plate	$7-9
Bicentennial mug, colored inside, ea.	$8-10
Bicentennial mug, white inside, ea.	$7-9
Revolutionary War plates, set	$50-60

Appendix III: Glossary

Assortment. The collection of individual items of a dinnerware shape.

Baker. An oval serving bowl.

Cable. General term used by many potteries in the early twentieth century to refer to plain utilitarian wares.

Connecting Line. A decorative line that runs along the verge and intersects a decal.

Coupe. A plain rimless shape.

Dapple. Type of gold decoration that is dabbed along the rims of dinnerware in an irregular fashion.

Decal. A print decoration applied over the glaze. The dish then goes through a decorating kiln where the decal "melts" onto the glaze.

Drop Line. Any trim that isn't on the edge, but falls very close to it.

Edge Line. Any trim along the edge. Also simply referred to as "trim."

Encasing lines. A set of two trim lines, one on the edge with the other towards the verge. They usually are on the outsides of wide colored bands decorating rims, hence the name, "encasing."

Encrusted. Term referred to decorations applied to gold or platinum bands.

Fade Away Trim. Colored trim along the edge that "fades" into the ware. Usually on the Versatile shape.

Grass Etch. A type of gold decoration where it is applied in thin brush strokes that looks like thin blades of grass.

Glaze. Hard glassy layer meant to protect the body of the ware. Glazes can be clear or in a solid color as in Lu-Ray or Pebbleford.

Muffin cover. A dome lid used on 8" plates. Their larger size and vent hole distinguishes them from round butter lids.

Nappy. A round serving bowl

Rose Mist. Dinnerware made of pink colored clay. It is given a clear glaze so the pink color shows through.

Silk Screen. An underglaze decoration where the color is passed through a screen that has been cut out in a specific design.

Sprig. A single decal. Most decal treatments are made up of a combination of sprigs in different sizes, but with the same style. Also called a "spray."

Two-tone. Also spelled "Tu Tone" in company records. It refers to the solid color thick band on Empire, Laurel, and Conversation that gives the ware a two-tone effect. Pieces may be completely glazed in a solid color to mix with decal ware resulting in a two-tone line.

Trade Sizes. A number system used by many potteries. For example, plates that would measure 10", 9", and 8" would be called 8", 7", and 6" respectively. Bowls and pitchers were commonly assigned numbers to judge sizes. The larger the number, the smaller the bowl. The 36s bowl found in most TST dinnerware gets its name from trade sizes.

Transfer print. A monochromatic underglaze design. The design is on a chrome roller that is given a colored glaze. The color is then rolled onto a thin sheet of paper, which results in a mirror image of the final print. The paper is then applied to an unglazed piece of pottery and the print "transfers" onto the ware. The piece is then given a clear glaze. TST's Chinese Temple, Delphian Rose, Center Bouquet, and Dogwood are examples of underglaze transfer prints.

Treatment. Any combination of decorative elements brought together to form a pattern.

Under-glaze. A decoration that is applied before the glaze. Silk screen, transfers, and most hand-painted work are underglaze.

Verge. The area of flatware where the rim meets the well. Also called the "ball."

Well. The center or flat area of a plate or platter.

Bibliography

Duke, Harvey. *The Official Price Guide to Pottery and Porcelain*, 8th edition. House of Collectibles, 1995.

Gonzalez, Mark. *An Overview of Homer Laughlin Dinnerware*. Gas City, Indiana: L-W Book Sales, 2002.

_____. *Collecting Fiesta, Lu-Ray and Other Colorware*. Gas City, Indiana: L-W Book Sales, 2000.

Meehan, Kathy and Bill. *Collector's Guide to Lu-Ray Pastels*. Paducah, Kentucky: Collector Books, 1995.

Sanford, Martha and Steve. *Sanford's Guide to McCoy Pottery*. Adelmore Press, 1997.

Spargo, John. *Early American Pottery and China*. New York, New York: The Century Co., 1926.

Stiles, Helen E. *Pottery in the United States*. New York, New York: E.P. Dutton & Co., Inc., 1941.

Whitmyer, Margaret and Ken. *The Collector's Encyclopedia of Hall China*, 2nd edition. Paducah, Kentucky: Collector Books, 1997.